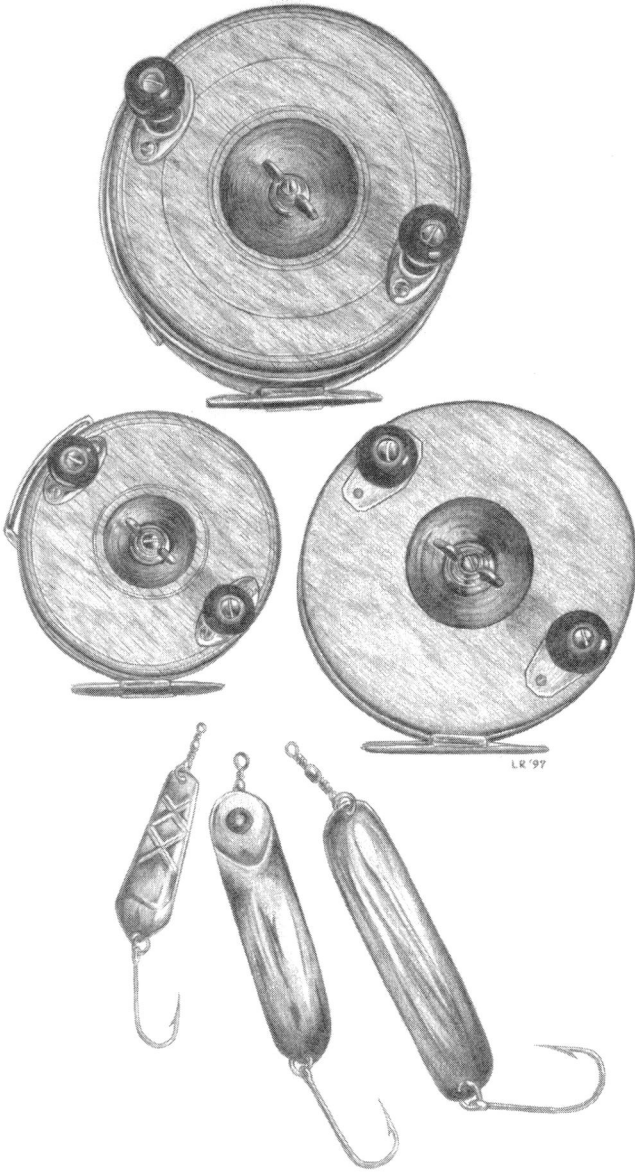

LR '97

PEETZ

A REEL FOR ALL TIME

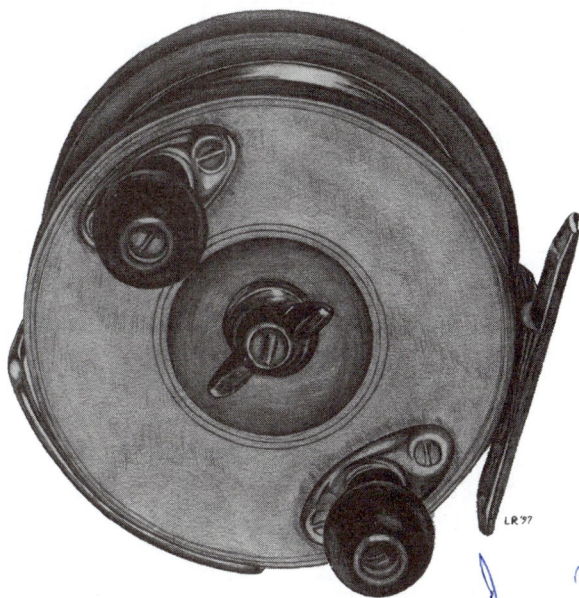

Douglas F. W. Pollard

Foreword by Alan Haig-Brown

Copyright © 1997 Douglas F. W. Pollard

CANADIAN CATALOGUING IN PUBLICATION DATA

Pollard, Douglas F. W., 1940-
Peetz, a reel for all time

ISBN 1-895811-48-1 Softcover
ISBN 1-895811-54-6 (Casebound edition)

1.   B.C. Peetz Manufacturing Company--History
2.   Fishing reels--British Columbia--History
I.   Title

HD9489.T334B36 1997   338.7'6887912   C97-910623-0

First Edition 1997

Heritage House wishes to acknowledge the support of Heritage Canada, the British Columbia Arts Council and the Cultural Services Branch of the Ministry of Small Business, Tourism and Culture and BC Parks.

Cover, Book Design and Typesetting: Darlene Nickull
Edited by: Rhonda Bailey
Original Artwork by: Loucas Raptis

HERITAGE HOUSE PUBLISHING COMPANY LTD.
Unit #8 - 17921 55th Ave., Surrey, BC V3S 6C4

Printed in Canada

To the memory of my father,
who caught his one and only salmon in Saanich Inlet.

Acknowledgements

This book would not have been written without the kind permission and support of the Peetz family. They probably did not expect me to probe so far into their lives. My very special thanks to Ola, Judy, Ivan and Betty, and Bud for their unhesitating help. I also received unstinting cooperation from the current owner of Peetz Manufacturing (1977) Ltd., Bill Hooson. His commitment has added two decades to the story of the Peetz reel.

Wherever I went in search of information I was given a warm reception. In Campbell River, Sandra Parrish, Archivist at the Museum, searched the Ron Francis tackle collection for me, while Ron and his wife Grace provided background to selected specimens, and gave me some insight into guided fishing in the locality. Joe Painter encouraged me to express my views on conservation, and willingly shared his thoughts on the state of salmon fishing. I am indebted to Joe's daughter Catherine for her advice; to Ken Enns and Ross Spires, long-time rowers of the Tyee Pool, who provided valuable information on reels used at Campbell River; and to Mike Rippingale, who guided Dr. Gavin Chisholm for many years.

Closer to home, I must express thanks to my friends Barry Stokes, Colin Funk, and Kevin McCullough of Victoria, each of whom provided me with useful documents and pieces of tackle. Jim Gilbert helped on the history of fishing in the Saanich Inlet. Stephen Rose, Secretary of the Victoria-Saanich Inlet Anglers' Association, kindly made records and trophies of the Association available to me. Stephen's grandfather John Rose gave me the rare experience of fishing Saanich Inlet with traditional Brentwood gear in his venerable boat, *Salar*. Bill Hoskyn added useful historical background on fishing in the Saanich Inlet. Rosemary Lupkoski provided background to the work of her late husband, Nick Lupkoski, who also made reels in Victoria. Donald Grant enlightened me with some new information on reel manufacture in South Africa.

I am especially grateful to Wendy Taylor, granddaughter of Boris Peetz, who gave my manuscript a thoroughly professional review. Her husband Doug can be credited with seeding the original idea of this book in my mind. Good friend Tim Bezanson provided a timely critique near the end. My talented fishing companion Loucas Raptis produced the delightful sketch heading each chapter. My brothers got involved too: Brian worked wonders on many of the photographs, while Martin advised me on suitable restoration methods.

Finally, a word for my dear and long-suffering wife, who encouraged me in my endeavors through the inevitable ups and downs of writing: thank you, Penny, for enduring solitude as I disappeared back into the depths of the manuscript.

Boris Peetz at work, 1951,
almost three decades after starting his first reel.

CONTENTS

LIST OF ILLUSTRATIONS

FOREWORD

The Harmony of a Wooden Reel

Nowhere in the world has beautifully worked wood been more closely associated with fishing than it has on the coast of British Columbia. From the intricately designed wooden halibut hooks carved by First Nations people to the graceful wooden plugs made by commercial trollers, the shaping and decorating of fishing gear has always been done with ritual and care. In fishing, the division between science and mythology is indistinct. Among fishing people, the two blend in "the-right-way." In B.C. for many decades, "the-right-way" for a sports fisher to bring in a troll-caught salmon has been with a beautifully crafted Peetz reel.

Forty years ago, in the late 1950s, I tried my hand at guiding salmon-fishing tourists in the Tyee Pool off the mouth of the Campbell River. In my training, a master guide showed me how to line up a spruce tree with a farmhouse to mark the point at which the gravel bar under the boat's keel curved in toward the shore. We rowed a 14-foot clinker-built Painter boat and talked about how the action of the rod tip tells what is happening with the flasher and plug; we spoke of the placement of the four-ounce weight on the line. And we spoke about reels. I loved the boat, the tide, and the experience of gliding over the bar on spoon-oared wings, but I was intimidated by the reel. By the need to have the tension set just right—tight enough so that when a fish struck, the line didn't pull off too fast and backlash, but not so tight that a poorly set hook would be pulled from the fish's mouth.

For me, the reel embodied the mysteries around the meeting between powerful fish in their tidal habitat and people in the surface-bound boats. There were wonderful things that went on inside that reel. And there was the sound, with all the urgency of a submarine's diving klaxon, when line was torn from the reel, when the guide was to yell to the surrounding boats, "Fish on!" It was an immeasurably rich world in which ritual, art, technique, timing, and tradition prevailed beyond the ken of my 16-year-old mind.

In this world I watched the landing of a golden-sided spring salmon in the late evening, the time when the sun's rays slant low over Vancouver Island to turn the glassy sea-surface orange and purple. When that great creature was laid out dead on a beach formed from gravel washed down over thousands of years from her ancestral spawning ground, there was always a hush. Sometimes the silence would be broken by the loud, gruff voice of a man uncomfortable with mystery, but in the best of times the hush was sustained while the sun's softness reverently brushed the fish's fading colors.

My guiding career was short lived, but the taste of that world and the morsels of knowledge that I gained have stayed with me and contributed to my experiences of tides and boats and beaches, from the Bering Sea to the Gulf of Mexico. And the connection I perceived between moving water and humans, as moderated through fishing reels, has grown to be an important part of my life.

When we humans connect with a fish, we are joined to a force that includes not only the fish, but the deep currents of the ocean, of time, and of our prehistoric memories. The honoring of that connection and our dependence on the salmon and their environs are things that the First Nations people show us are in need of great ritual.

Over the years, I have watched the ritual of landing a fine tyee being replaced by a feeding frenzy that bespeaks the greed of those who would exploit mystery for personal gain. Even as responsible citizens warn of collapsing stocks, some resorts advertize how many fish can legally be killed in a day. Happily—and we must hope it is not too late—other resorts encourage guests to come for the experience of a relaxed day in a boat and an evening watching the sun change the color of the sea. If we are to reaffirm the experience of fishing over the killing of a dock full of fish, then we will reaffirm the rituals that bring harmony to that experience—be they for a parent and child in a mail-order aluminum boat or a wealthy tourist in a custom cruiser.

In his definitive work on the Peetz reel, Doug Pollard reminds us that the use of simple tackle can enhance the experience of fishing. He shows us how the Peetz reel became the blend of science and mythology that makes it the traditional "right-way" to troll for salmon on the West Coast. Pollard records the sale of the family business to Bill Hooson in 1977 as only being confirmed when, "Ivan and Judy Peetz were eventually convinced by Bill that he could and would preserve the tradition, reputation, and quality of Peetz products." That commitment is an example for us all.

Peetz, a Reel for All Time is a remarkable book that takes us a step further toward linking our shared human experience with salmon to the ongoing traditions of the First Nations, who have successfully provided stewardship to the salmon runs over the millennium.

Alan Haig-Brown
August 1997

PROLOGUE

Escaping west from the grip of Ontario's lingering winter one April, I was lured into an evening of fishing in Saanich Inlet. My companion was trying out his latest fishing accessory, a downrigger. We trolled a green hootchie at 120 feet down the middle of Finlayson Arm. My rod suddenly went slack and then bent into something solid and very much alive. After I entertained fellow anglers with my antics for half an hour, Dick netted a magnificent salmon, and we scooted back to Hall's Boathouse. It was my first chinook. It tipped the scales at 22 pounds, quite ordinary for the Saanich Inlet, but the biggest fish I had ever landed. I remember that fish very well. And I can still hear the reel, a big raucous Nottingham that positively barked as the fish tore off line. The reel was a Peetz.

Fishing tackle is marvelous stuff, and older reels have a particular magic. Their functional beauty, fashioned in wood, brass, and aluminum alloys, tells of a less hectic past when it took hands as well as machines to make the instruments of our sport. This is not to deny the fine lines and workmanship of quality tackle made today. Nevertheless, classic reels have many admirers, and they command prices that can bring gasps of astonishment at auctions. There was a big gasp last winter at a British auction when a single Hardy Perfect sold for £17,000, not including a 10 percent commission.

Despite the enormous popularity of angling, there are few books dealing with the history of fishing tackle. Those that exist tend to focus on the better-known makes of Great Britain and the United States. Canada is rarely mentioned. Most of the famous names have disappeared. Yet on Canada's West Coast there still exists a solid core of tackle manufacturers that are rooted in the fabulous salmon and trout fishing of this part of the world. The name Peetz is undoubtedly the best known.

After moving to Victoria—a decision not entirely unconnected to the events related above—I was slow to realize that the reel that roared on that seminal occasion in 1976 was something rather special. The

Peetz reel is unique in a world of angling that has become big business. By adhering to basic materials and principles, it has managed to survive the onslaught of imported space-age graphite and alloy paraphernalia. It is one of the very few wooden reels that are still being produced to catch fish. It does so admirably. Of far greater significance, Peetz reels, and other sturdy pieces of tackle manufactured under this name, have left their mark on the development and traditions of sport fishing on Canada's West Coast.

The various owners of the Peetz company have maintained the integrity of design and materials that Boris Peetz put into his prototypes over seventy years ago. Peetz reels are simple and tough. They have given years of reliable service to many thousands of anglers. The number of salmon taken on Peetz reels is incalculable, but at times could well have exceeded the combined catch on all other reels on the West Coast.

The company and its past are on my doorstep. Once the idea surfaced, writing this book became irresistible. As I set about my task, my intention was simply to document the evolution of these rugged masterpieces. However, as my notes began to accumulate from interviews with the family, the current owner, and other local personalities, I realized I was into something more than a collector's guide. Here was an intriguing story of entrepreneurial doggedness that insisted on preserving a tradition in the face of many difficulties. While "they don't make them like they used to," this company very nearly does. I also discovered a hard core of traditionalists. There are people who still enjoy using simple tackle in the pursuit of fish; they have something to offer at a time when our sport and its resources are in trouble.

I have tried to capture the story of the Peetz reel and the people who made it, at the same time paying some attention to detail for the collector. This is by no means the definitive account of the many variations extant, and I suspect that there are some important early models that I have missed. A comprehensive collection of reels has yet to be assembled. If I manage to stimulate interest in what has been Canada's most successful tackle maker I have succeeded in my mission. If the reader derives even a fraction of the pleasure I have from writing the book, I shall be fulfilled.

Doug Pollard
Victoria, BC

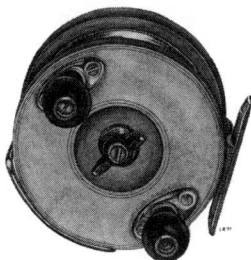

CHAPTER 1

Introduction

It is raining as I write the first lines of this book. October has been dry, but with the month drawing to a close the rain has finally come. It has been raining almost continuously for three days.

Rich forests of firs and cedars in the hills around Victoria are finding relief from the summer drought. First the mosses and then the underlying humus became saturated. Now rain is penetrating the soil. It will take most of winter to recharge deeper layers that will be pressed into service again next summer. Yet the forest is patient, and is already releasing some of the precious fluid.

Percolating through the forest floor, along passages and galleries left by long-decayed roots, the water gathers into rivulets to feed the Goldstream River below. The river is swelling visibly, and over the next few weeks it will be bursting with activity, leaving life and death in its wake. As many as fifty thousand salmon, mostly chum, will take possession of its gravel bed for their final act. The act has been repeated over countless generations.

Promoted locally as a wildlife spectacle, the Goldstream salmon run disguises a tragedy that has unfolded in the deep fiord beyond the river's estuary. For until recently, Saanich Inlet was spectacular in its own right. It boasted a sport fishery that rivaled more famous destinations on Vancouver Island.

Long before Europeans and others arrived here, the Tsartlip people built communities along the Inlet and lived off its abundant salmon, lingcod, and shellfish. European settlers found a reliable feeding ground for salmon of all ages that provided marvelous fishing year round. Second-year coho—bluebacks—could be counted on in spring, chinook abounded through summer, and fall produced magnificent mature coho that could be taken with a surface fly. Later, anglers were to discover

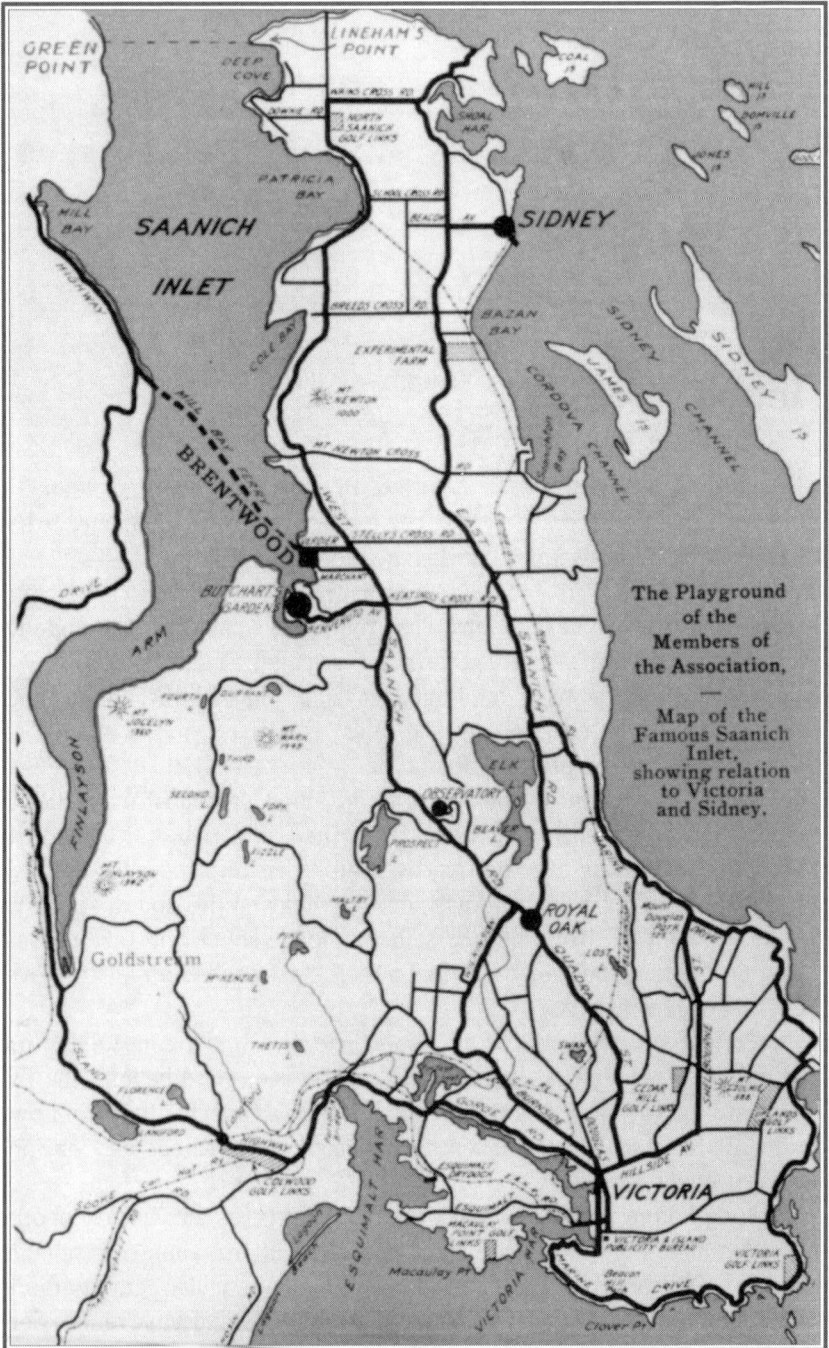

Fig. 1.1. Saanich Inlet, reproduced from the Fourth Annual Year Book of the Victoria-Saanich Inlet Anglers' Association (VSIAA), 1935.

superb winter fishing for chinooks in the Inlet's sheltered waters. Brodhurst, Creed, Gilbert, Harrap, Ireland, Stacey, and other names hung over boathouses that catered to the fishery.

Bruce Obee tells us how the Inlet was yielding 25,000 salmon a year when Harry Gilbert's son Jim stopped guiding in 1970. Annual catches of up to 20,000 were made even in the mid-1980s, and Brentwood fishing guides could still make a modest living. By the end of the 1980s the fishery had collapsed. The recorded catch for 1994 was 1,111 fish. Harrap's Boathouse is now a waterfront restaurant, with kayaks for hire. A once-familiar fleet of colorful clinker-built rentals no longer dots the water-scape.

What went wrong in Saanich Inlet is still open to question. It has received its share of insults from industrial and residential developments. Yet a few fish—indeed large fish—are still taken by persistent and knowledgeable anglers. The Goldstream run remains healthy, and includes a few coho, chinook, and steelhead among its spawners.

Not all the enterprise nurtured by the Saanich Inlet met the same demise as fishermen's boathouses. The survivors included a remarkable company that for more than seventy years has produced fishing tackle whose name is practically synonymous with the West Coast sport fishery. The company took its name from a Russian-born immigrant who arrived in Canada in 1910. That person was Boris Cecil Peetz.

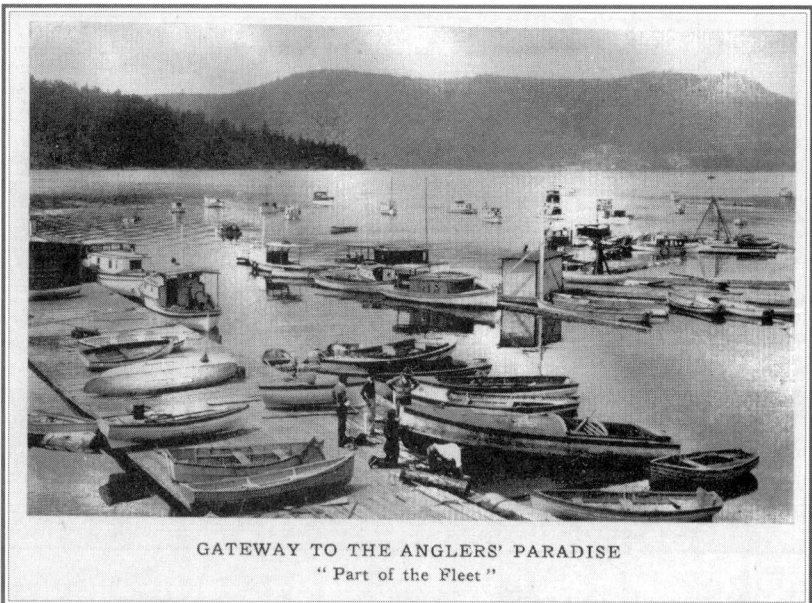

GATEWAY TO THE ANGLERS' PARADISE
" Part of the Fleet "

Fig. 1.2. From the VSIAA 1935 Year Book.

Fig. 2.1. An accomplished craftsman when he arrived in Canada, Boris doubtless had little idea, as he sat at this Victoria tea party, that his future lay in fishing reels.

Chapter 2

Boris Cecil Peetz

To begin the story of the Peetz reel we must leave the West Coast and travel east. Beyond British Columbia, beyond Canada, and even beyond Nottingham, in England, although later we shall visit that place of genesis. We must focus the mind's eye first on Russia in the late nineteenth century, when that great country was bursting with art and science.

Tchaikovsky and Rimsky-Korsakov were composing the music we love today. Rachmaninov and Skryabin were entering manhood. Stravinsky and Pasternak were still children. As Pavlov developed his profound theories on conditioned reflexes, the scientific world rejoiced at the genius of the great chemist, Mendeleyev.

Yet all was not right in Russia, for behind the plethora of talent lurked bureaucracies of unimaginable incompetence, and a populace steeped in misery and despair. Misguided policies and poor harvests resulted in two famines in the 1890s, which left millions starving and seeded riots among the proletariat. Despite its powerful grip as the motherland, Russia was a discouraging place for creativity to flourish. For historian Edward Crankshaw (see Bibliography), the fate of Mendeleyev, dismissed from his University chair on a trumped-up charge by a mediocre Minister of Education, epitomized the roots of decline that has seen little relief since.

Boris Peetz was born in Moscow in 1883. His name is not typically Russian. The family may have been among the thousands who migrated from the Low Countries into Germany and European Russia in the late 1700s. It seems unlikely that his parents were other than working class (a term without official sanction in Russia). They had different backgrounds, his mother Russian, and his father of German descent. A builder, his father was probably relatively well paid. But the young Boris could not have escaped exposure to the turmoil in his country, even in the somewhat insulated society of Moscow. By the time he had reached his teens, word was out that a better life could be had elsewhere in the new century ahead. Boris got caught in a wave of migration that would take millions of Europeans westwards.

At the age of seventeen, he left Russia. His subsequent movements are not known with certainty. He may have spent time at schools in Berlin and Poland before moving on to England. It was probably in England that Boris trained in silversmithing. Eleven years after leaving Russia, Boris moved again. This time he traveled to Canada. Arriving by steamship in Montreal in 1910, he began to apply his trade of silversmithing at the Argus works of the Canadian Pacific Railway.

It is hard to imagine the contrast Boris would have found between his native home and the young Canada. The Trans-Siberian Railway project had been soaking up that country's resources at a phenomenal rate when he departed from Russia. Boris would have found the Canadian transcontinental railway project well developed. The CPR was at the height of its expansion. Its dynamic president, Julius Van Horne, had seen a new opportunity for capitalizing on the wealth generated by the industrial revolution. Those who could afford to travel were looking for adventure, but in comfort. The CPR supplied it. At strategic points along its track, the company had built magnificent hotels that were transforming Canada into a tourist destination of world renown. The West was particularly enriched, with grand edifices in Calgary, Lake Louise, Jasper, and Banff.

Anxious to become the focus of western commerce, the City of Victoria had eagerly accepted a bold plan for its inner harbor, with the Rattenbury-designed Empress Hotel as its centerpiece. The Hotel had opened in 1908, just three years before Boris arrived in Canada. An immigrant himself, Francis Rattenbury was giving a remarkably elegant aura to the young city, with the Parliament Buildings and, later, the Crystal Gardens flanking the regal Empress Hotel. That elegance, which remains to this day, attracted wealthy elements of a North American public seeking some respite from the unrelenting wilderness around them.

As intended, Victoria became a fashionable destination for Canadian, American, and European tourists. A grand tour of the West, whether by rail or by steamship, was incomplete without a suitably long stop at this decidedly Victorian outpost of the British Empire. The city's character was also influenced by itinerant British subjects who were heading home, or taking a break from duties elsewhere, or simply deciding that Victoria was a better place to live.

Victoria's growth and the expanding aspirations of the CPR created enormous opportunity for skilled trades people, and the temptation to move west got the better of Boris within a year of his arriving in Canada.

Fig. 2.2   Earliest known work of Boris Peetz: a plated spirit kettle for his travels across Canada in 1911.

In 1911 he boarded a train bound for Vancouver. Among the belongings he carried that day was a small copper kettle and spirit stove that he had made specially for the long transcontinental trip. Now in the possession of his daughter Judy, the little kettle (Fig. 2.2) gives us a glimpse of the ingenuity and self-reliance that were to become personal hallmarks of Boris Peetz.

On reaching Victoria, Boris may have tried to re-establish himself at the Empress, but he would have learned that the hotel's needs in silver-smithing had already been contracted to a local company, Challoner & Mitchell. In any case, he saw that silversmithing was becoming highly mechanized, and decided to apply his craftsmanship to jewelry repair. He first worked with the Redfern jewelry store, but soon transferred to Wengers Ltd. on Yates Street.

It was not long before domestic developments took charge of his life. Shortly after his arrival he met Muriel Edna Brame. Edna was an English girl from Harborne, near Birmingham. As was not uncommon at the time, she had left home in her late teens to travel. She lived among families in Hungary as a teacher and nanny for two years. Her travels continued with a friend, this time to Victoria, and there she met and married Boris.

While struggling to establish themselves in business, Boris and Edna bought three lots on Tulip Avenue, then on the edge of town. With their own hands they built a house that would be their home for the next seventeen years. They lived in a tent while the house was under construction, and Edna gave birth to their first child, Ola, under canvas. As if they had time to spare, they installed a lawn tennis court, and hosted tennis and bridge tournaments for their rapidly expanding circle of friends. Over the coming years they would enlarge the family with Sybil (Judy), Ivan, and Anthony (Bud).

Within a couple of years Boris established his own business in jewelry repair and manufacture at 654 Yates. He must have been a hard man to track down sometimes. The Victoria Business Directory shows a different business address almost every year until the late 1920s, including several on Yates, Fort, and Douglas Streets. It is hardly surprising that errors crept into the Directory, but Boris must have been particularly chagrined by the 1920 edition: his name had slipped from "Jewelers-Wholesale" to "Junk Dealers." Suffice to say this was remedied in the following edition.

While at Wenger's, Boris had met a watchmaker by the name of William Hall, and they later shared premises at 1229 Langley Street. Their friendship grew over the coming years. From time to time, Bill invited Boris and Edna and their family out to his summer home on Coles Bay in the Saanich Inlet. Boris and Bill went fishing for salmon while their children played in the garden. They began their exploits in the local manner: they used handlines.

For a year or two Boris and Bill paid out lines of linen cuttyhunk weighted with rocks, sometimes fifteen pounds of them. They also tried leaded lines, on which weights were molded around the line at short intervals. A length of inner tube tied between the boat and line cushioned the impact of a heavy strike. They fished together through the summer from Bill's boat, and caught many salmon. While handlining was effective it was also strenuous, and hard on Boris's dexterous hands. Yet it was while using this simple method that Boris became captivated by fishing. The experience was to alter the course of his life.

By 1926 the two friends had moved from Langley Street to premises at 613 Yates. A year later they had relocated, Boris to 1206 Douglas and Bill to 1239 Broad Street. Boris was still listed as a jewelry manufacturer. But the seed of a new enterprise had been sown. The first Peetz reel was already three years old.

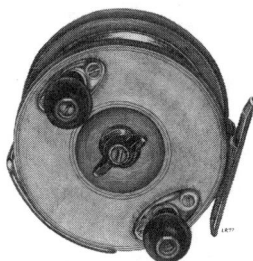

CHAPTER 3

The First Reel

A sport fishery had been evolving on the West Coast for several decades before Boris and Bill began hauling in salmon. Van Egan tells us how the phenomenal fishing at Campbell River got world attention even before the turn of the century.

The publicity started in the prestigious British country magazine, *The Field*, in 1896, when Sir Richard Musgrave described his catch of a 70-pound tyee. In the ensuing years, he and others continued to report on spectacular fishing in and around Campbell River. More reports appeared in *The Field* between 1906 and 1908. The number of visiting anglers grew accordingly, as did the number of guides, boats, and other facilities for them. But the sporting men and women from abroad, equipped with the best available tackle and suitably attired in Harris tweed, were hardly role models for the majority of West Coast residents, many of whom were preoccupied with the art of survival.

The vast majority of salmon taken until the late 1920s were caught commercially by hardy souls determined to eke out a living from the sea. These fiercely independent people could be found up and down the coast, often far from canneries which would pay as little as a cent a pound for their hard-won catch. They trolled handlines from small skiffs, rowing for perhaps fourteen hours a day.

In his account of the hand troller, Hubert Evans tells us how an experimentally minded fisherman by the name of Tom Rogers caused a minor revolution in the late 1920s. Rogers fished off Hornby Island, south of Campbell River. Discarding his handline-trolled lure, he still-fished a live herring from a bamboo rod fitted with an imported walnut reel. Hard rowing was now only necessary to reach the fishing grounds and return; once in position, the skiff could be held with the minimum of effort. Rogers was mooching. His catches were noticed by fellow fisherman. Many changed to his method, but the advantage was not long lived. Seine nets and mechanized trollers would soon spell the end of the solitary fisherman rowing his skiff from dawn to dusk.

The transition from handline to rod and line would have far more impact on recreational fishing. In 1924, a group of enthusiasts established the now famous Tyee Club of British Columbia. Their aim was simple and ambitious: to promote a sporting approach to the world-renowned salmon fishing in Campbell River. Rules and awards were created to reinforce the underlying concept, and have changed little to this day. Van Egan notes that the founders of the club, convinced that angling was more sporting and more satisfying, set out with the intention of converting the many handliners to rod and line. Evidently they were highly successful. In 1922 seven out of eight recreational fishermen in Campbell River used handlines. In 1926, just two years after the Club's founding, the handliners had been reduced to one in seven.

Although it had quickly assumed the title of Salmon Capital, Campbell River was by no means the only place to fish for salmon. Victoria was rapidly gaining a reputation for good fishing off the Oak Bay and city waterfronts, and excellent catches were being made in Saanich Inlet. Boris and Bill were probably several years ahead of the local Campbell River anglers in their conversion from handlines. Sometime during their early fishing ventures, Boris Peetz and Bill Hall acquired rods and reels and began to appreciate the challenge offered by big salmon.

As he became more familiar with the Inlet, Boris turned his attention to the particular problem that it presented to anglers. A mile and a half out from Brentwood, the bottom plunges to a depth of over 700 feet, near the mouth of a deep channel known as Finlayson Arm that reaches south to the Goldstream River, The prized chinooks were to be caught at depths down to 200 feet or more. But fishing at even half this depth was not without its problems, and it called for a long line, heavy weights, and suitably robust rods and reels.

Reel capacity was particularly challenging because at least 600 feet of line, and preferably 900 feet, was needed to reach fishing depths and to contain the run of a big fish. The line used, cuttyhunk, was a carryover from handlining; the only alternative was solid copper wire. Both were bulky and quickly filled a typical 5-inch reel. The reels of the day were either imported Nottinghams or American multipliers. Boris leaned towards the simple Nottinghams, handsomely turned in walnut, cherry, mahogany, or beech.

Initially, Boris Peetz modified imported reels to suit the local conditions. He fitted heavier brass and fiber washers for the drag, and a longer spindle to accommodate them. A more robust reel was clearly needed. Applying the skills of his trade, Boris set about constructing a reel for the

Inlet.

Judging from the remarkable consistency to be seen throughout the evolution of the Peetz reel, we might have expected the first model to be a rugged version of the Nottingham. But in the opinion of Bill Hooson, current owner of Peetz Manufacturing (1977) Ltd., the earliest known reel was built along the lines of a Scarborough.

The characteristic feature of the Scarborough reel is the absence of a back-plate. A check is awkward to fit without a back-plate. The spindle is mounted directly onto a bracket that extends the foot placement over the perimeter of the drum. It is a simple reel, being only slightly more complicated than the spoke reel used by Chinese anglers for centuries (see Buller and Falkus 1994).

The Scarborough reel takes its name from a seaside town in York-shire, England. It was here, in the early 1920s (just at the time Boris Peetz was experimenting with his own reels), that a tackle dealer by the name of Pritchard began to develop reels for sea fishing along the rugged north-east coast. Pritchard saw advantages in the absence of a back-plate apart from minimizing the cost of manufacture. The line has little to catch on in the cast, and a fast-running drum can be readily controlled by hand. He produced reels in wood and Tufnol (a Bakelite-like material, used as an insulator base in radios, for example). Different styles, commonly from five to eleven inches in diameter, were made for beach casters and boat anglers. It was probably Pritchard who took the Scarborough to the peak of efficiency with the "oil-bath," a magnificent Tufnol reel whose spindle ran on bearings immersed in pressurized oil. Without a check or drag, the "oil-bath" demanded some skill if over-runs were to be avoided, but the casting distances attained were prodigious. Some anglers took to the cliffs and cast into unfished waters hundreds of feet below.

While most Scarboroughs were made of wood or Tufnol, Hardy introduced a particularly fine version, the Natal, in alloy and brass, for sea fishing in South Africa. The Natal first appeared in 1924, and was followed by a smaller (4½-inch) version, the Filey (named after the resort town south of Scarborough). So popular was the Scarborough design in South Africa, especially along the Natal coast, that a small tackle industry emerged in much the same way as the Peetz company. Keith Palmer built Scarboroughs in wood until 1952, when he changed to fiberglass. Even today, Moulded Fibre Glass Products, on Natal's South Coast, still produces Scarborough reels; their DeLuxe model is faced with wood. Meanwhile, the Seareels company of York continues to manufacture Scarboroughs in a material similar to Tufnol, and only ceased their production in hardwood in 1996.

Fig. 3.1. Early extension handle on The Pacific Reel.

Some traditionalists still use wooden Scarboroughs, and have created opportunities for craftsmen. In his workshop at Garforth, near Leeds, Dennis Mann turned out eighty reels in his first year, 1996, in a variety of English hardwoods, from eight to ten inches in diameter. Dennis could be the only person outside the Peetz company who is currently producing wooden reels in commercial quantities.

Scarboroughs have always been large. Their size was driven by needs for line capacity and rapid line recovery. The same needs were felt by the anglers of Saanich Inlet, yet it was probably the simplicity of the Scarborough that led to its becoming a model for the first Peetz reel. Boris may have seen English reels, and he certainly would have seen American models. Some versions of the all-metal Pflueger Captain were built in the Scarborough style; others were built without backs but had the spindle mounted directly through the foot, causing the reel to sit across the rod handle rather than hang under it, as is conventional today.

The earliest reel in the collection of Peetz Manufacturing (1977) Company had a 5¼-inch drum turned from a single piece of wood. It was finished in black enamel, had a single extendible handle that could be locked in the extended position (Fig. 3.1), and a line guard attached to the strap (Fig 3.2). It had no check. Rudimentary wings were attached onto the retaining nut of the spindle. There was no lock screw. The strap

Fig. 3.2. Earliest known Peetz reel: The Pacific Reel, 1924.

was ribbed and stamped with the words "THE PACIFIC REEL PAT. PEND-ING".

The pressed brass strap and foot assembly shows Boris's knowledge of metallurgy. He designed it to take advantage of the relative stiffness of pressed brass compared to cast brass. Set at right angles to the strap, the foot required a strong connection. Boris solved this with a combination of solder and rivets, a feature that would endure until 1959 when the company acquired a punch press that would combine the two components in a single piece of metal. Virtually all imported Nottinghams of the time had strap and foot cast in a single piece, and many of them bent under stress. On the other hand, most of the early Scarboroughs I have seen have a foot that is braised and riveted in place. The original Pacific Reel may well have been inspired by an imported reel of this type.

Although the company refers to its beginnings in 1925, there are indications of a few Pacifics being sold in 1924. Even these would not have been the first reels Boris built. It is hard to pinpoint the exact year, let alone the day, but we can surmise that, one morning in the early twenties, he rowed out into Saanich Inlet, and the first of countless salmon was taken on a Peetz reel.

CHAPTER 4

From Nottingham to the Pacific

On the face of it there is not much in common between fishing reels and Belgian lace. Nevertheless, fancy tastes in the nineteenth century for this particular luxury led to the emergence of the modern center-pin reel.

The wealthy and not-so-wealthy of Europe had created a huge demand for delicate lace to adorn hats, skirts, windows, and dinner tables. When the industrial revolution hit the English Midlands, Nottingham's entrepreneurs built mills to mass-produce what had formerly been handcrafted. Nottingham had already built a reputation for hosiery in a large-scale cottage industry. Now it flourished as England's lace center.

Doing what comes naturally during time off, some mill workers took to the local River Trent and fished for roach, dace, and the larger pike and barbel with the crude tackle of the day. A few would have purchased the clumsy wooden winches and brass reels available at the time, but these were either small or heavy to use. In any case they were beyond the pocket of most anglers. Metal reels, in particular, could not be made without a substantial investment in machinery. More seriously, their heavy spools had too much inertia for casting and "long trotting" light float tackle. More than one worker would have recognized the possibilities in wooden bobbins at the mill as they spun off miles of lace.

What happened next has been summarized from Henry Coxon's article in the September 7, 1895 edition of the *Fishing Gazette* by Graham Turner. It would appear that a Joseph Turner was the first to transform the wooden bobbin into a smooth-running fishing reel. His creation was soon taken up by others, including William Brailsford. The popularity of fishing along the Trent alone was probably sufficient to sustain the local tackle industry, but then "Nottingham George," a.k.a. George Holland, took the Brailsford reels to the River Thames. The demand for his

"Nottinghams," which were superior to anything available in the south of England, simply exploded.

Despite a new-found popularity for Nottinghams in the south, it was in the industrial Midlands and the north of England where huge markets unfolded, and where fishing tackle diversified at a phenomenal rate. For all its simplicity, the Nottingham became the foundation for some of the greatest innovations in angling equipment. One of the most significant emerged around the middle of the nineteenth century: the drum was fitted with a latch that engaged with a groove in the spindle. The drum could now be separated from the spindle with a simple squeeze of the latch, instead of removal of a lock screw and nut. John Stephenson emphasizes a much more important result of the latch: instead of bearing on washers at the base of the spindle, the drum could now spin on a pin-like tip of the spindle. The so-called "center-pin" was exceptionally free running, making it ideal for long trotting, casting, and quick retrieval. Stephenson distinguishes between Nottingham and center-pin reels, although he shows a page from a 1910 J.W. Martin catalogue which refers to center-pin Nottingham pike reels.

The center-pin was adopted for a variety of reel types. One of these was the Hardy Silex. For almost a century, the Silex has enjoyed a special place in British Columbia as the steelheader's reel. Few would associate this highly refined machined reel with the lowly Nottingham, yet the Hardy Silex takes its roots from the Nottingham Silex, a walnut center-pin with a Silex action that first appeared in 1899; the latter is another example of a Nottingham center-pin.

The Sheffield Pattern was a Nottingham variant whose drum had been hollowed out to reduce weight. This was important for match or competition fishing, where large purses depended on speed in casting and retrieval. The idea of weight reduction took a quantum leap forward with the introduction of the spoked drum, which Turner attributes back to Henry Coxon. It continued to be developed primarily under the name of Allcock. From behind, the Coxon Aerial offered in 1896 looks like an ordinary Nottingham, with a brass star-back set on a walnut back-plate. The reel evolved in metal to culminate in what was probably the finest center-pin ever produced, the 4-inch Match Aerial No. 9053. The Match Aerial was made in 1939 only; World War II interrupted further production, and, tragically, bombing raids destroyed all the tools and dies being stored in Birmingham. Books by Graham Turner and John Stephenson, from which I have drawn much of the above information, contain a wealth of detail on the history of British and other fishing tackle, and are recommended for further reading.

John Orrelle's book on fly reels also provides useful background to the center-pin, from which, of course, the fly reel developed. As an American author, Orrelle uses the term "single-action" to describe reels other than multipliers and fixed-spool. Thus Nottinghams, center-pins, Scarboroughs, and fly reels alike can all come under the umbrella of single-action reels. Useful as it is, the term is not widely applied in Britain, where it is more likely to refer to the mode of action of the check.

Turner describes how, in 1878, George Holding applied for a patent for a modification that would revolutionize the world of angling: the reel seat was mounted on a small turntable that converted a simple Nottingham to a temporary fixed-spool reel. Three years earlier, a patent for a device that achieved the same effect had been granted to two Americans, Thomas Winans and Thomas Whistler. The spool of their metal, horizontally mounted reel could be flipped up on a hinge to face the rod's axis, allowing line to fall away freely in the cast. But it was a simplified form of Holding's reel that a Scottish angler developed and sold on a large scale: the Malloch Sidecaster. In 1899, Illingworth went back to the mills to devise the first true fixed-spool reel, by winding the line around a fixed, stationary spool, in the fashion of a bobbin.

Foreigners invaded the ancestral home of the Nottingham. By the 1970s the once-contemplative coarse angler had discarded the versatile center-pin reel. Fixed-spool and spincast reels took its place. Thus equipped, a child can cast a float across the river with ease, and will catch more fish into the bargain. There is nothing intrinsically wrong with more fish being caught early in an angler's career. But such precocious ability has a price. The skill demanded by a center-pin is never acquired, and thus never savored. The link between angler and float or fish is dulled by gears and clutch.

Some anglers have abandoned reels altogether. The ancient roach-pole has been resurrected, in astonishing lengths of forty feet or more. The price tag on a modern graphite pole would make even a flyfisher blanch. As we shall see later, the center-pin is staging something of a comeback in Britain. The unplanned renaissance results largely from attempts by one Christopher Yates to portray the lighter, philosophical side of fishing.

The basic center-pin did not catch on in North America. The main reason was that the quarry were of altogether different species from those in Britain, calling for spinning and crank-bait casting rather than light float and ledger tackle. The Kentucky multiplier had established pre-eminence among freshwater anglers. Only with fly tackle did the British

Fig. 4.1. A Scarborough-style reel fitted with an experimental check.

manufacturers make significant inroads into the huge market of freshwater angling in North America.

It is a little surprising that North American reel manufacturers did not exploit the magnificent wealth of hardwoods on their doorstep. A collection of old tackle catalogues gathered together by Melner and Kessler featured just two wooden reels originating in North America between 1839 and 1931. These were the horizontally mounted Good Luck reel, patented on March 9, 1897, and the Auto Reel, a wooden 2:1 multiplier manufactured by Kleinman of New York. According to the H.H. Kiffe Company of New York, the former was available in no less than thirteen models, from five to eight inches in diameter, with different woods (mostly mahogany), finishes, handles and ball-bearing options.

On both coasts, but especially the West, a market niche existed for larger Nottinghams. Thousands of reels by Allcock, Hardy, Heaton, Milward, and a host of other tackle manufacturers were imported during the first half of the twentieth century. Although often reinforced, inside and outside, with rings, stars, and straps of brass, few were up to West Coast conditions. Some woods and finishes simply could not withstand prolonged exposure to salt water. Line capacities were often inadequate. But the critical weakness was in their drag system, which could not provide proper tension for holding heavy weights and controlling strong fish.

Just how and when the early Peetz reels developed remains somewhat conjectural. Family recollections are hazy, for all the children were quite young during this period. Fortunately, as will be seen, we do have unequivocal documentation of a sophisticated reel being offered for sale

Fig. 4.2. Strap and check button on early Nottingham Peetz reel.

in 1935. Given Boris's careful approach, amply demonstrated over the following decades, and the advanced form of the 1935 reel, a decade of prior development does not seem unreasonable.

Boris did not continue with the Scarborough-style Pacific for long. While simple to manufacture, it had its drawbacks. For one thing, fitting a check proved to be awkward. The Peetz company maintains a collection of their reels that attest to a period of experimentation and trials. In one example, a circular metal case was attached to the strap, centered on the reel's spindle. An external button actuated the check pawl, which was held in a circular spring (Fig. 4.1). A 4-inch Bakelite reel of similar design was later produced by Ebro, while the Australian company Alvey produced a comparable though massive 9-inch model in marine plywood. Boris may already have had in mind a much more sophisticated addition for his reels. He would need a full back to house its mechanism. He would have to resort to the traditional Nottingham style.

For whatever reason, the Depression years offer little information for reconstructing early development of the reel. Records of production from that period are almost nonexistent. But we can be sure that the ingenious and energetic jeweler was experimenting with reels, with or without

Fig. 4.3. Later extension handle on all-wood drum of early
Nottingham-style reel.

a market. It is highly probable that significant steps were made before the Depression, but the year of his first Nottingham-style reel is as yet unknown.

The earliest known specimen in the company's collection heralded a design for what would become the flagship product of the company. The reel has a wooden back-plate, but retains the spindle bracket in the form of a straight brass strap (Fig. 4.2). A threaded hole at the tip of the spindle would have accepted a lock screw. The 6-inch drum was assembled from two separately turned pieces of wood held together by six brass screws and painted brown. It has a single extendible handle, almost certainly of more recent origin (Fig. 4.3). The check closely resembles that installed in imported Nottinghams of the time: a brass caliper spring, held in place by two screws. The optional check engages a coarse, 12-toothed gear inside the drum. The pawl is actuated by a large brass button on the back-plate that is virtually identical to that used today. Few of these reels have survived, for they still lacked some of the essential robustness of later designs.

By the time the Depression hit Victoria, Boris was in his late forties. He continued to produce and repair jewelry, but his eyesight had deterio-

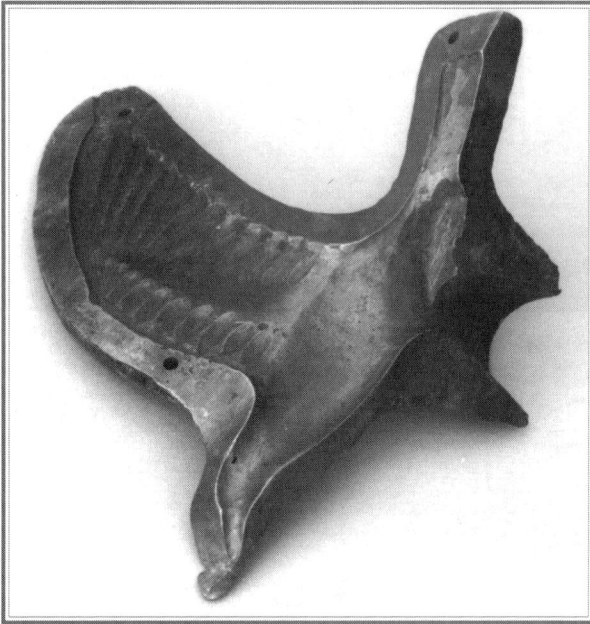

Fig. 4.4. Part of a mold for a seagull car emblem.

rated to the point where fine work was unduly demanding. He would try his hand at almost anything that might make money to support his growing family.

The rapid escalation of car ownership provided new opportunities. Around 1930, he became an *avant garde* recycler, setting up the Universal Mats company on Blanchard Street for the business of turning used automobile tires into doormats. However, after a year or two of operations he ran into a patent conflict with a Vancouver competitor. Curiously, the final outcome, while not in his favor, left him with some financial compensation. He did manage to patent a design for manually operated turning indicators for cars, but they quickly became obsolete with the advent of an electrical system. For a while he turned his jeweler's craftsmanship to the production of emblems for car hoods (Fig. 4.4).

In Harry Gregson's account of the Depression years we learn that 12,000 of the area's 40,000 inhabitants were on relief by 1932. Unemployment ran at 50 percent. Building permits dropped by over 80 percent. The Empress had more staff than guests, even after cuts. Despite such statistics, Victorians were better off than most. A community spirit emerged. People helped each other. Gregson remarked on the self-sufficiency of Victorians: they kept gardens and they fished.

An inveterate survivor, Boris must surely have seen the opportunity presented by the Depression. A modest investment in fishing tackle could help to keep a family nourished indefinitely. Who needed jewelry when they were hungry?

Even before the Depression was over, thoughts began to turn to travel. By now Boris and Edna had been in Canada for over two decades; it was time to visit the family. But it was Edna's family, in Harborne, that they would visit, and in September 1932 they embarked on the SS *Ascania*, with younger son Bud, for a three-month trip. Just before their departure, Boris made a remarkable discovery. He had had practically no contact with his family since leaving Russia, but now he learned that his brother Michael also had left Russia. He, too, had emigrated to England, where he went into business, eventually to run a cosmetics company by the name of Kraska. Bud has but hazy recollections of meeting his uncle.

According to Bud, the trip was financed with the compensation package that had been awarded after losing the conflict over mats. We can only speculate today, but it seems inconceivable that, once in England, Boris would not have been drawn into tackle shops. And he could have hardly failed to realize that Redditch, home of Allcock and other noted tackle manufacturers, lay only twelve miles to the south of Harborne. It is tempting to speculate further that he settled on the final design for his reel as a result of the trip.

There was one major change to be made before the Pacific Reel began its remarkably steady course over the next sixty years. The all-wood construction of the drum did not withstand the rigors of trolling. It was inclined to distort under prolonged pressure. The solution was simple: the inside wood face of the drum was replaced with a tempered brass plate that could be modified or replaced as needed. The same construction had been used extensively in imported Nottinghams. In retrospect, we can see the advent of the metal-backed drum clinched a design that has endured for over sixty years. The plate differed from those found in most English reels: a step in its dished profile increased substantially the line capacity of the drum at the cost of very little extra weight.

While Boris seems to have settled on the caliper check design quite early, he appears to have tried at least one other style, perhaps after his trip to England. Jim Gilbert showed me something quite unusual from his collection—what is almost certainly a Peetz reel with a straight check spring. In common with the patented Ebro, the pawl is actuated by a lever-type button when the latter is turned through 90 degrees (Fig.4.5). It is possible that a patent conflict led to his adopting the final check design. The drag nut is round, and the remaining handle-plate is diamond shaped (the reel also has a retrofitted extendible handle; see Fig

Fig. 4.5. This early 6-inch Peetz features an unusual lever-type check button which rotates the pawl against a simple spring wire inside.

4.6) but in other respects the reel has a standard Peetz finish, including a brass drum-plate.

Since all subsequent reels have the brass drum-plate, the question arises, what are the identifying characteristics of the earliest reels with this feature? Again, I refer to a reel in the company's collection. It is only in detail that this 6-inch reel differed from later models. The most conspicuous feature is the wood, which is varnished oak. The handle-plates are clearly hand-cut, flat, with a step to accommodate the knob's spindle nut. A domed D-washer engages a flat filed onto the spindle; it is held in place by a handmade wing nut that resembles a bird. This elegant drag nut can be found in early postwar reels also.

The check's components may be the most useful indicator of age. A hand-forged caliper spring is held in position by a simple fold of brass, and grasps a check pawl that is also mounted on a small piece of brass. The check button is identical to those in later reels. The check assembly is attached to the wooden back-plate by domed steel screws, rather than brass.

My own collection includes a similar reel that may be made of beech. Unusual wood may indicate that a reel is of the early type. Used alone, it is not a conclusive indicator, for a variety of woods were tried in years when mahogany was in short supply.

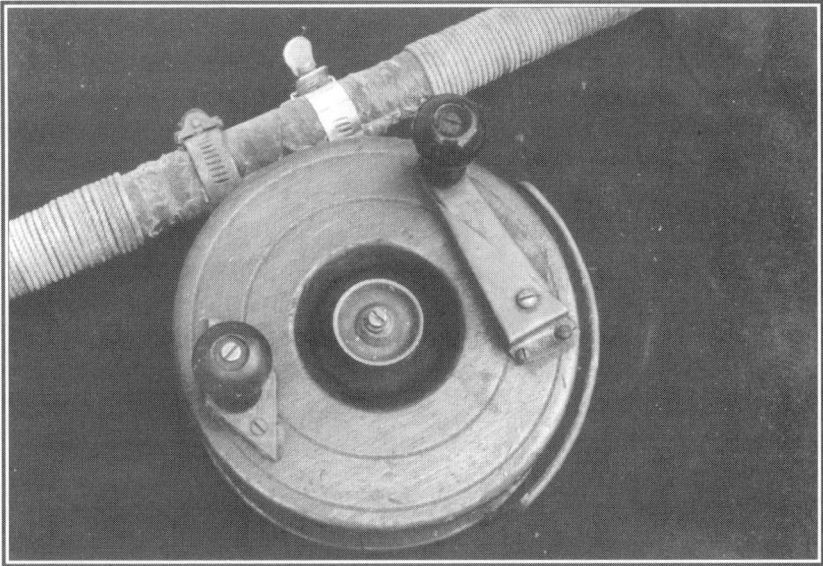

Fig. 4.6. The drum face of the reel includes an extendible handle.

Word spread about the new reel and other products. Requests began to arrive, not only from local anglers but from guides and resorts outside Victoria. If production was to meet orders a small factory would be needed. The 1935 British Columbia Directory showed a new address for the company: 572 Johnson Street.

It is hard to be sure when Boris finally decided to commit his talents and enterprise wholly to the manufacture of fishing tackle. Bud Peetz recalls pondering over a form that he was required to fill out at school in 1939: even at that late date he could not decide whether he should state his father's occupation as jeweler or tackle maker. Years before, circumstances had caused Boris to shift from silversmithing to jewelry manufacture. After years of preoccupation with jewelry, had he at last found his life's calling?

We can get a little insight into the answer to this question from an interview he had in 1951 with L.G.Temple of the Vancouver *Sun*. Boris reflected thus on his move from jewelry to fishing tackle: "Making fishing tackle appeals to me more than making trinkets. Jewelry is only ornamental, while salmon lures are both ornamental and useful, like boats!"

Some of his creations could hardly be called trinkets. He built a magnificent miniature of the SS *Elginshire*, in solid silver, for the retirement of one Captain Crawford of Vancouver. His craftsmanship was recognized by the City of Victoria. He was invited to make a silver casket containing the key to the City for William Butchart, founder of Victoria's

Fig. 4.7. Hookum, Chinook, and V lures (top to bottom).

Butchart Gardens; he made a similar key and casket for Lord Willingdon, Governor General of Canada. It would not be the only Peetz product to pass to a representative of the Crown.

With materials and metalworking skills at his fingertips, Boris loved to experiment with new tackle, especially lures and weights. By the early 1930s, he had perfected three new salmon spoons: first the Chinook, and then the Hookum and V lures (Fig. 4.7). They were made in several sizes, and each was available in different finishes.

A # 7 Chinook measured a full 6 inches in length. It was sold in solid brass and solid German silver (a colorless form of brass); both polished and matte finishes were also available. Some were hand-painted.

The Hookum was a particularly handsome spoon, with a striking copper "eye" soldered over the swivel connector. The # 7 was 5½ inches long. Many Hookums were painted, and were available in brass and German silver. Some of the early Hookums were silver-plated by local silversmiths (anglers, of course) and have been eagerly sought by collectors.

The Vs were smaller lures, the # 7 measuring 4¼ inches. Their characteristic feature is a pair of Xs, impressed in the tapered body. Some Vs were painted red.

The Abalone lure was crafted from abalone shell. Carefully shaped and buffed, the Abalone came close to being angling jewelry.

A remarkably simple release mechanism was designed to shed disposable weights from the line as soon as a fish was hooked (Fig. 4.8).

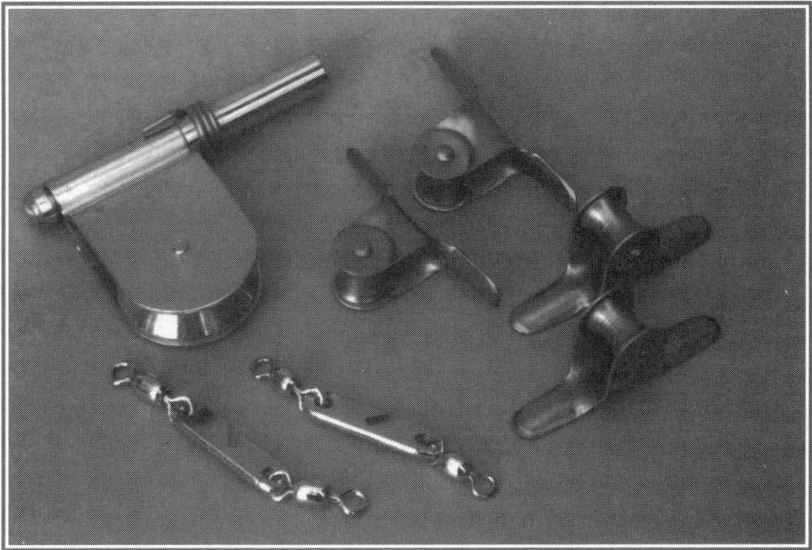

Fig. 4.8. Patent roller guides, and trip swivels that jettisoned disposable weights.

The fish could then fight unencumbered by pounds of rocks or scrap metal. Years earlier, Boris and Bill Hall had invented a wire-mesh bag that would release its load of rocks when triggered. Patented sliding lead sinkers became a major item of manufacturing, and whole-cane rods appeared under the Peetz label. Fishing tackle had finally emerged as the core line for the company.

The barrel swivel, a small item essential for trolling and spinning, was by no means as easy to make as its simple appearance would suggest. It took no less than five machines to prepare and assemble the parts. One of them was a monster, incorporating 12-foot girders, and crankshafts and flywheels stripped from Model T Fords. It was one of several innovations that would help to establish his fledgling tackle company. A swivel was needed at the leader end of every spoon. The great machines continued to churn them out by the tens of thousands after the second world war, to the extent that for several years the company was listed in the British Columbia Directory as having "fishing reels and swivels" as its main lines of business.

The first official mention of the new enterprise occurred in the 1935 Directory, when he listed his business as "fishing tackle." But by then he had launched an innovation that would make his name a legend in West Coast fishing. He was offering something that the deep-water angler had only dreamed of—a reel that measured line.

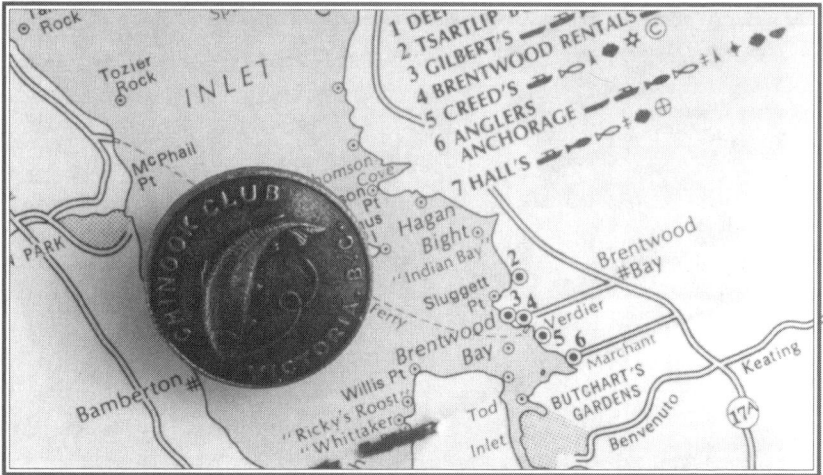

Anglers' Association

Club Trophies

The Buttons are made in three different metals, viz., Bronze, Silver and Gold.

Bronze Button.— For the capture on tackle as specified under rules and regulations published herein, of a Spring Salmon weighing 20 pounds or over.

Silver Button.—For the capture as above, of a Spring Salmon weighing 30 pounds or over.

Gold Button.—For the capture as above, of a Spring Salmon weighing 40 pounds or over.

Championship Award.—For the capture of the largest fish of the year. A diamond added to the button.

Awards will be made as soon as Investigation Committee approves claim.

Trophies won by visitors will be forwarded by mail to any part of the world.

The winning of a button makes the holder a member of the Chinook Club for life.

Fig. 5.1. The Chinook Club button, bearing the insignia designed by Boris Peetz, became a symbol coveted by all Saanich Inlet fishers.

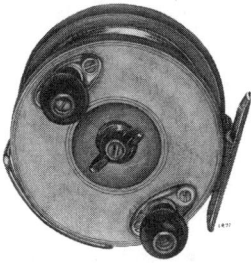

CHAPTER 5

A Reel That Measures Line

The Depression notwithstanding, sport fishing had become a major business around Victoria. After all, quite apart from being excellent food, a salmon was a highly desirable commodity, and could be bartered for all kinds of goods and services. Also, the fishing was attracting visitors from further afield.

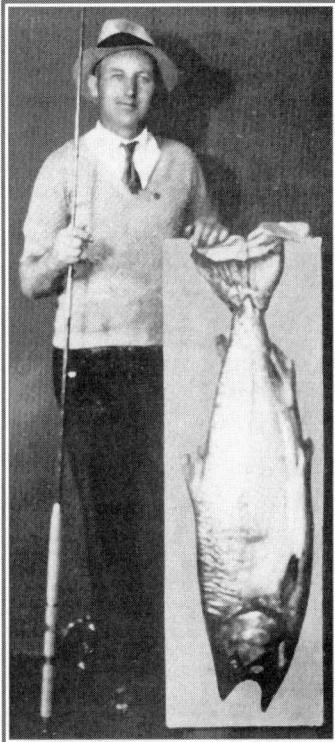

In 1932, local anglers organized the Victoria-Saanich Inlet Anglers' Association, whose objectives, among others, were "to induce visitors to come annually to enjoy the sport of salmon fishing, and try for trophies, and to make Victoria their headquarters" (Anon 1932). The Association got off to a good start, for the very first trophy fish entered was a 53½-pound chinook, caught by Roy Thompson of Victoria on June 12, 1932.

A Chinook Club was formed within the Association to recognize anglers who caught trophy fish. As in the Tyee Club, membership had to be earned. Trophy buttons (Fig. 5.1) recognized chinooks according to their size: bronze for fish over 20 pounds, silver for fish over 30 pounds, and gold for fish over 40 pounds. A diamond added to the button for the largest fish of the year became the

Fig. 5.2. 1934 diamond and gold button winner, F.E. Guest poses with his classic wooden reel and his 45 lb. trophy salmon.

Championship Award. (Fig. 5.2) The buttons were comparable to those issued by the Tyee Club in Campbell River, but the weight classes were ten pounds lower. Boris Peetz, an early member of the Association, designed the buttons. They were stamped out on his newly acquired drop hammer (buttons for the Tyee Club were supplied by Birks Jewelers). Boris donated the Hookum Cup for the largest fish of the season caught by a junior member. (Fig. 5.3) There was another trophy donated to the Association by a tackle maker. Allcock and Co. Ltd. of Redditch, England, donated the S. Allcock Perpetual Challenge Shield for the winner of a series of fishing competitions in the Inlet. (Fig. 5.4) Later, Boris contributed the Peetz Annual Trophy, to recognize the largest fish caught by a new member of the Chinook Club (Fig. 5.5).

Yearbooks of the Victoria-Saanich Inlet Anglers' Association provide fascinating glimpses into Saanich Inlet in its glory. For example, from Thompson's first fish in 1932 to October 1934, the Chinook Club issued 135 trophy buttons. It is evident from photographs in the books that many of these were caught on Peetz reels.

The B.C. Peetz Manufacturing Company advertised in the yearbook to promote its Chinook and Hookum trolling spoons, abalone shell and grilse spoons, and Pacific fishing reels. The company's small advertise-ment (Fig. 5.6) in 1935 included an item of special interest to the col-lector. The Pacific Recorder, "the only reel made that registers the length of line being used," was offered at $10.00 for a 6½-inch reel. Clearly, the Pacific reel had made significant strides over the previous decade. It had become a sophisticated trolling reel, available at a reasonable price. It cost more than English imports, which were typically $6.95 for a 5-inch reel, but it was an altogether tougher and bigger reel, and featured the unique line indicator.

The Recorder was an immediate success. Anglers could now quickly and precisely return their lure to depths where fish were feeding. Line could be let out or wound back at will, without having to count pulls or turns. But even the massive proportions of the Recorder were inadequate to deal with an irritating problem of weed. At some point in the 1930s, the Saanich Inlet became infested with a seaweed known locally as "Japweed." It was generally believed the weed was introduced with Japa-nese oysters. Devices were fitted on boats to catch the weed before the fishing line sliced into it. The line still became festooned with the stuff.

Boris's solution to the added weight of weed was to give his reel more cranking power with an extendible arm to one of the handles. When not in use, the arm was closed by a spring, and the handle was restored in its normal position. In theory the angler would not be ex-

Fig. 5.3. Originally known as the Hookum Cup (after the Peetz "Hookum" trolling spoons), this Peetz Cup was won by a young Bobby Redgrave in 1937. The cup is shown here with the winning Mahatma Gandhi lure.

Fig. 5.4. A gift from Redditch, England, the Allcock Trophy, bore near its base a true angler's supplication.

"Lord suffer me to catch a fish
So large that ever I
When speaking of it afterwards
Shall never need to lie."

Fig. 5.5. An attractive trophy designed to honour a club newcomer, the Chinook Club Peetz Annual Trophy. A 1952 silver crest (right) on the Chinook Club Trophy bears the Peetz hallmark.

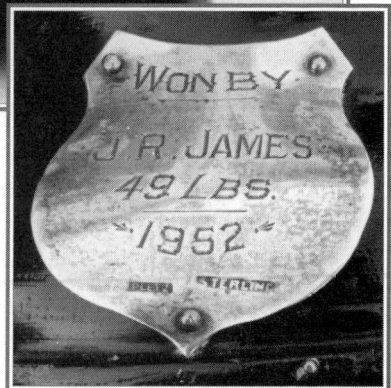

Fig. 5.6. A revealing advertisement from the 1935 Victoria-Saanich Inlet Anglers' Association Year Book.

posed to a dangerous, flailing lever when a fast-running fish took off. A fixed handle was still there for playing fish, while the crank effectively doubled the radius of the other handle. The crank handle was available on 5- and 6-inch models, and is still available, although the primary reason for its use has not arisen for many years.

An early form of the extendible handle had a circular lock nut instead of a spring for holding the handle in position. Its presence on the earliest known reel suggests that the desire for more cranking power arose before the arrival of Japweed. The raising of baskets of rocks and other heavy weights required considerable effort, and an extendible handle would have been appreciated. However, the spring-loaded type was inclined to fly out when a fish ran fast, with painful consequences for unwary hands. The problem would be countered later by Ray Deall and others who built the "Oak Bay Special." The Special had a 9-inch disc of 1/4-inch Plexiglass screwed to the face of a 6-inch Peetz; this permitted much wider spacing of the handles (Fig. 5.7).

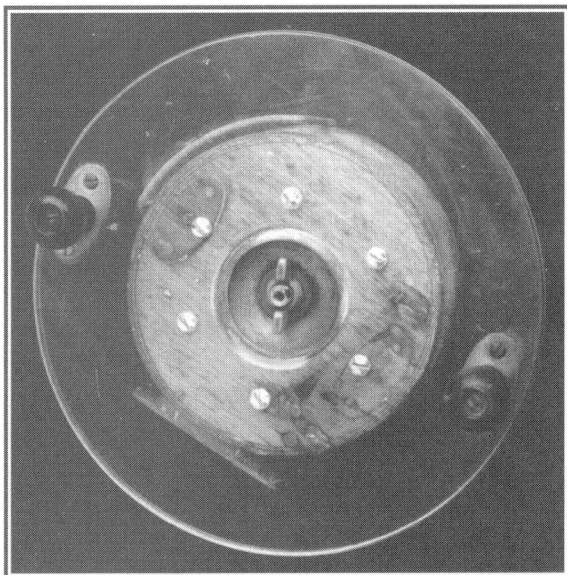

Fig. 5.7. The Oak Bay Special was a Peetz reel modified to provide leverage.

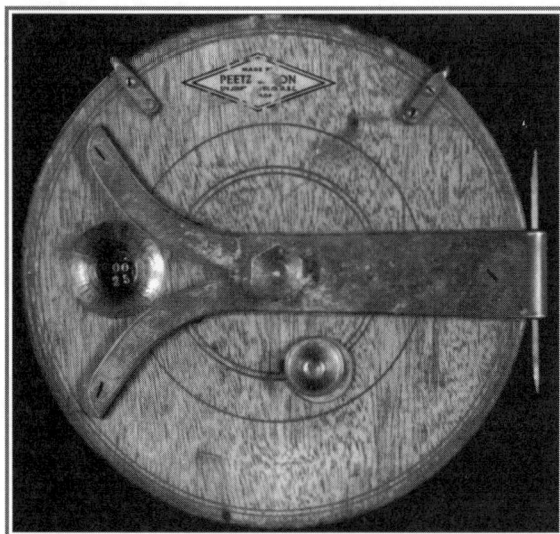

The early Recorders were very distinctive, featuring a brass strap split into a "Y," with the window of the line register between the arms of the "Y" (Fig. 5.8). A 6½-inch Y-strap Recorder in my possession measures up to 600 feet at 25-foot intervals, and I have seen another that is identical. This is a magnificent reel

Fig. 5.8. Back-plate of the Y-strap Recorder.

worthy of a place in any tackle collection.

The elegant Y-strap was Boris's method of adding strength to the large, thin disc of mahogany that formed the back-plate. The back-plate was also reinforced inside with a ring of brass around its perimeter, and an irregularly cut piece of sheet brass that secured both the indicator mechanism and the check.

Fitting a check mechanism into the Recorders had presented something of a problem. Earlier reels employed the classic brass caliper spring that could be found in practically all imported wooden reels of the Nottingham design, and that is used to this day by the Peetz company in all its non-recording reels. The caliper spring embraces the reel's spindle between its two arms. It could not be fitted into the big Recorder's back-plate because of the substantial mechanism driving the indicator disc. Boris devised a new spring. Contracted into a crown-like shape, it was set to one side of the spindle, opposite the recording mechanism (Fig. 5.9). Some 2½ inches across, it was almost ½ inch wider than the caliper. But the radial dimension of the check assembly had been reduced by a full inch.

The Recorder is much loved by Peetz adherents. The reel was and remains handmade. But it is hard to imagine the amount of labor that was put into early Recorders. Their mechanism was massive. Some of the parts were taken from bicycle hub gears. Two worm gears, one on the drum, and one on the transfer shaft, were made from wire wound and soldered onto the axis by hand, and filed down to drive toothed gears.

Fig. 5.9. Early (left) and later mechanisms of 6¾-inch Recorder reels, both with aluminum discs.

An aluminum disc that rotated to indicate the length of line out had its numbers punched in by hand at properly calibrated positions. Lengths in 25- or 50-foot intervals appeared in a small window in the back-plate as line was let out.

At some point in the late 1940s, the Y-strap gave way to a simple tapered strap. The entire inner surface of the back-plate was lined with sheet brass, bounded by the brass ring. The indicator disc appeared in at least two forms. The earlier type, fitted to Y-strap reels, was a single disc with a drive gear fixed to its center (Fig. 5.9, left); the disc was black, with metallic numbers. The later type was formed from two superimposed discs. The inner had teeth around its perimeter which meshed with the transfer worm drive (Fig. 5.9, right); the outer disc displayed black numbers on a metallic background. The transfer mechanism of the later model was lighter in construction. Except for the disc, it has remained basically unchanged to this day. The disc has been made of plastic for almost five decades.

It is still difficult to establish the age of early Recorders with certainty. The presence of an aluminum disc is a clear indication that the reel was produced in the 1930s or 1940s. My own reel of this era is of the earlier type (single disc) but bears a "Peetz and Son" decal, suggesting manufacture after the elder son Ivan officially joined the company. But Ivan had been with his father before and, on occasion, during the war. He suggested to me the decal might have been used before the war. Or it may have been put on at a later date if the reel had been returned for servicing; the decal is not an entirely reliable indicator of vintage.

Ivan Peetz chuckled when he recalled how he got free mooring for his boat *Seafarer II*. Art Hall, who ran Hall's Boathouse at the mouth of the Goldstream River, argued that the Recorder reel could not possibly determine line length accurately. He reasoned that as the line was fed out, the effective diameter of the core diminished and hence let out less and less line for each turn of the reel. Ivan asked Art if he would give him a month's free mooring if the Recorder could be shown to be accurate. Art agreed and Ivan proceeded to pull out line along a measured length of slip. Sure enough, the Recorder measured out perfectly, and Ivan got his mooring. The Recorder's disc had been calibrated as measured lengths of line were wound onto the drum.

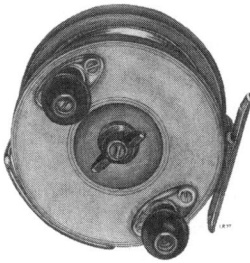

CHAPTER 6

Big Reels, Small Reels

By the mid-thirties, the big Recorder had found its niche in the local fishing tackle market. It was the reel of choice for those trolling very deep waters, for it had both capacity and the unique line register. Other companies tried to capture some of the growing market for large-capacity reels. A Victoria sports store advertised a new "Chinook Reel" in the 1935 yearbook of the Victoria-Saanich Inlet Anglers' Association (Fig.6-1). Wilson and Lenfesty professed to be sole agents for the product of what was probably a small manufacturer on the West Coast. The Chinook was a well-finished Scarborough reel; its 8-inch drum was mounted on an imported Allcock bracket.

The 6½-inch Pacific Recorder was a heavy reel, weighing as much as five pounds when fully loaded with wire line. It had been designed for the Saanich Inlet, and for this it was ideal. Few inshore waters are as deep as the Inlet, however; it happens to be the only fiord on Vancouver Island's east coast. The reel was not universally accepted. In Campbell River, for example, most fish were being taken on imported equipment. These included popular American multipliers, which had already achieved a high degree of sophistication in response to the demand from big game fishermen. Such reels could also

Fig. 6.1. A revealing advertisement from a 1935 yearbook.

be very expensive: Zane Grey's big game reel, custom built by Hardy, cost a reputed $7,000 (before the war). Clearly, the Peetz reel was in an entirely different class, but if it was to be a mainstay for the business it would have to appeal to more than the members of the Victoria-Saanich Inlet Anglers' Association.

Even as he launched the Recorder, Boris Peetz had a suite of new reels in mind. His advertisement in the Association's 1935 yearbook gives no clue as to what was on his mental drawing board. Around 1938, he moved into larger premises next door. Number 574 Johnson Street was destined to become a landmark for coastal anglers for the next thirty-five years. But the demand for fishing tackle was suddenly interrupted with the outbreak of war in 1939. Canadians departed for overseas service, and the supply of raw materials was virtually cut off.

Boris persevered with his creations. Occasionally he could be found rummaging around Victoria dockyards, looking for suitable pieces of dunnage. He was planning for happier times ahead, when people would get back to the important things in life, like fishing.

The war brought an end to imported Nottinghams from England. Boris could not keep up with the local demand for trolling reels. Necessity being the mother of invention, the shortage drove others to apply their skills on the lathe. Machinists in the Victoria dockyard began turning pieces of oak and mahogany into functional reels. The "dockyard specials" were mostly of the Scarborough design, with drums mounted directly on a cast brass frame that incorporated the strap and foot in a single piece. They were unmarked. Some have a stamp under the bracket that indicates the reel size. They can be found in 5-, 6-, and 8-inch diameters. One name would emerge from the dockyard after the war: Nick Lupkoski had applied his own interpretation of the Nottingham, and would be selling his reels long after hostilities had ceased.

As the war drew to an end, Boris began to think about family matters. Ola had married and left for eastern Canada, not to return until 1964. After working next door at Jeune Bros., Judy had joined the WRNS. Ivan was serving in the Navy, reaching the rank of Chief Petty Officer. Ivan's transfer from patrol boats operating around Victoria tells us something about one of the company's future principals, and also about the government's way of handling problems. Incensed by the poor quality of repairs his boat had received, Ivan wrote a strong letter to headquarters, condemning the offending boatyard. Very soon afterwards he was on his way east, to serve in the North Atlantic. He made several runs from his base in Londonderry, and was in the flotilla receiving a surrendered German Navy. Bud had gone to university during the war, but his studies were interrupted when he too joined up. Among the more fortu-

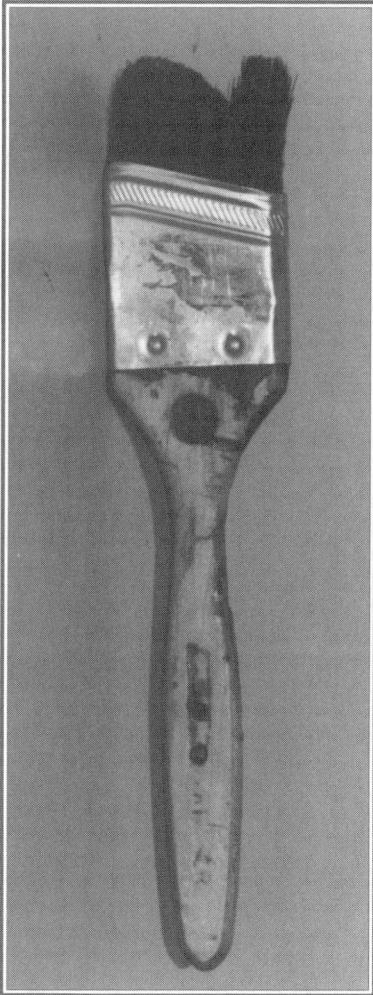

Fig. 6.2. The brush that varnished more than 150,000 reels.

nate, although he did not think so at the time, he saw little action as the war drew to a close.

Before the war, Ivan and Judy had spent many hours in the Johnson Street shop, engaged in the multifarious chores of fishing tackle production. With peace restored, the business officially became a family affair, as Ivan joined his father and the name changed in 1947 from B.C. Peetz Manufacturing Company to Peetz and Son. (Although, as noted in the previous chapter, the "Peetz and Son" decal may have been used earlier.)

The new company title soon became something of a misnomer, as Ivan was joined by Judy and Bud. Judy left for a year at MacDonald College, but returned in 1948. Her earlier experience in the shop now began to pay off. She made thousands of rods, first of whole Calcutta cane, later of fiberglass. She also finished and assembled reels; mahogany drums and back-plates were carefully filled before being treated with at least two coats of varnish. Marine spar varnish was preferred over more modern but less durable lacquers, which did not stand up well to salt water. The present company office displays an ancient brush, worn to the profile of a reel drum, attesting to applications on 150,000 reels (Fig. 6.2). Bud acted as the company accountant, worked on tackle production, and improved the design of a number of items, including the check spring.

The enlarged company began to promote its tackle with a brochure (which can be dated between the years 1949 and 1953 from the Victoria telephone number E-3652). A Y-Recorder appears on the cover, but inside we learn that two Recorders were now available, a 6¾-inch model for lines measuring up to 900 feet at 50-foot intervals, and a 5¾-inch version for lines up to 600 feet, also at 50-foot intervals.

The larger Recorder appeared little changed from the prewar model, although at 6¾ inches it was now nominally a quarter-inch larger in diameter. Those I have seen measure 6½ inches in diameter. Not all situations called for the capacity of the 6¾-inch reels. In many locations, salmon were to be found at moderate depths, certainly less than 100 feet. They could be reached with shorter, lighter lines and lighter weights. After the war, new materials emerged from which fine lines could be made. As we shall see, they were not without problems. Production of the big reels was not to last long.

The 5¾-inch Recorder required another modification to the check. The crown-shaped spring was too wide to fit into the reel's back, and it was left to Bud Peetz to find a solution. Soon after joining the company in 1949, Bud designed a butterfly spring, in which the spring's arms were crossed and given reverse curves to hold the check pawl. The compact spring, measuring only 1½ x 1½ inches, was held in place directly by short screwed pillars, instead of with the traditional hand-cut brass plate. This new spring was fitted subsequently into the 6¾-inch reel for the last few years of its production (Fig. 5.9, right). It is still fitted to Recorders.

The company's collection includes a small Recorder fitted with an aluminum disc. It is a 5-inch reel with a two-piece, perimeter-driven indicator disc. I have not found any early advertisements or other documents mentioning this size. Nevertheless, a few 5-inch Recorders were produced in later years; they were fitted with plastic discs. For a brief period there may have been three sizes (5-, 5¾-, and 6¾-inch) in production. Ultimately, the 5¾-inch (nominally a 6-inch) Recorder would become the flagship product of the company.

A small photograph in the postwar brochure illustrates four other reels (Fig. 6.3). These are referred to as Standard trolling reels (lacking the Recorder feature), and were offered in 4-, 5-, 6-, and 6¾-inch sizes. To the casual eye the first three are indistinguishable from those being manufactured in the final years of

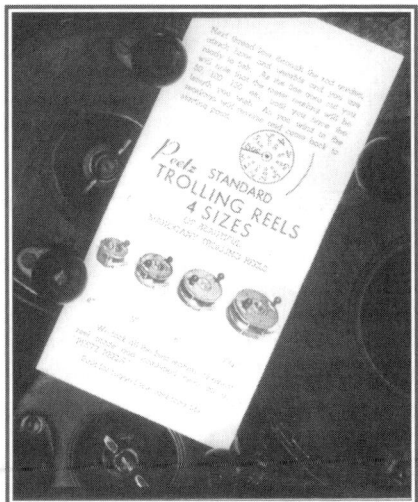

Fig. 6.3. Brochure illustrating four Standard reels, 1949.

the twentieth century (now known as models 1400, 1500, and 1600 respectively; the 6-inch Recorder has become the model 2500).

After the war, bucktailing became very popular on the West Coast. It is an exciting way to take saltwater coho. Large streamer flies, traditionally of dyed deer or polar bear hair, are trolled in the bubbling wake of a boat. Coho are usually located below feeding seabirds, especially gulls. With luck, a pass over such spots results in a wrenching hit that sends the reel screaming. Sometimes the fish can be seen finning on the surface. The headlong charge of a finning 10-pound coho gets adrenaline surging even before the fish smashes the fly. The technique requires sufficient line to contain the long initial runs of a heavy fish. Two hundred yards of light line does not require a large reel, and the 5-inch Standard reel became a popular choice for local bucktailers. In Campbell River, the 5-inch reel gathered adherents among trollers as well as bucktailers, for its capacity was adequate for the relatively shallow waters of Discovery Passage.

The 5-inch Standard reel has quietly assumed its place in a piece of Victoria's fishing history. Over the past thirty-five years, Bob Wright has put together the largest fishing resort corporation in North America, the highly successful Oak Bay Marine Group. The Group's estate includes world-famous Painter's Lodge. Like most enterprises, it started in a modest way, with the acquisition of the MV *Lakewood*. Since 1962, the 61-foot *Lakewood*, now renamed MV *Discovery Princess*, has been plying the waters off Oak Bay. I made my first Pacific catch, a 20-pound lingcod, from the *Lakewood* in 1972. Twice a day during summer, people of all ages board for a fishing and sightseeing trip into Haro Strait. Tackle gets heavy and rough use, especially from first-time anglers. Except for a short period, the reel of choice has always been the 5-inch Standard

Fig. 6.4. This mouthy rockfish looks capable of swallowing the Peetz reel that helped land it.

Fig. 6.5. Five-inch Peetz reels by the dozen help provide a traditional fishing experience aboard the MV Discovery Princess.

Peetz (Fig. 6.5). Other reels were tried for a couple of seasons, but could not match the local product for durability and ease of maintenance.

Just what prompted Boris to produce the 4-inch reel is not clear. In Ivan Peetz's view, the compact little reel was just too much work for bucktailing, where lines had to be wound in frequently as weed gathered on the fly. He suggested that it was the result of Boris's thrifty nature. The large initial cuts taken out of expensive planks of mahogany left chunks of wood that would have bothered him. A range of manufacturing sizes, five in all, would offer more complete utilization than a lesser number, especially if small dimension pieces could be used. In spite of this possibly expedient origin, the 4-inch reel was quite popular, as is indicated by the number in today's market.

Apart from its overall size, the 4-inch reel was similar in construction to the larger reels. The wooden back-plate was somewhat thinner and the strap and foot were proportionately smaller; the usual caliper check mechanism was employed. Despite its smaller diameter, the drum maintained a generous width, with handles of the same size used on the 5-inch reel. The reel had a slightly chubby appearance. Like the larger models, it was robust, easily able to withstand the normal knocks that

boat tackle receives, especially from well-paying but inexperienced clients.

Over a period of several years, the entire line of reels was subjected to slight but progressive reductions in the number of models available, and in their dimensions. Both 6¾-inch reels were dropped, and the 6-inch Standard reel was reduced to 5¾ inches. Intermediate diameters can be found; it seems likely that their essentially handmade nature allowed for quite wide tolerances at the lathe that imparted an element of individuality to each reel.

All Standard reels produced since the war have been reinforced with a ring of brass inside the back-plate, in the fashion of the first Recorders. All 5¾-inch Recorders have been reinforced with a tightly fitting disc of sheet brass over the wood.

The smaller Recorder was produced for several years. It was nominally a 5-inch reel, and differed only in size from the larger reel. Only a few hundred were sold. Today the 5-inch Recorder is a highly desirable acquisition for those collectors aware of its existence. In the 1970s, Ivan Peetz refined the 5-inch for light lines (see later); it would be the last step in the evolution of reels before the company finally passed from the family.

While it had its origins with thick cuttyhunk and solid copper lines, the Recorder reel was ultimately calibrated for use with 60-pound (20-gauge) monel line. Because they are almost inelastic, metal lines impart a very direct feel when playing a fish, and are still preferred by some anglers of the old school. Metal lines are very hard on normal line guides, and will render them unserviceable after a short period of use. Boris proceeded to develop roller guides and tips for his rod (Fig. 4.8); eventually they were patented.

The swivel-making machines continued to spew forth swivels by the thousand. But perhaps the most successful of all his inventions was the sliding lead weight, for which he was awarded a patent in 1947. There are literally hundreds of tons of lead on the reefs and ocean floor around Victoria, strewn in small pieces bearing the word "Peetz" on their sides. Twenty-ton deliveries of pig lead from the smelters in Trail were normal at Johnson Street.

The early weight was triangular in profile, with a clip of brass wire at its front into which the fishing line was pressed (Fig. 6.6). The clip would hold the weight well clear of the lure or flasher, but would release it when jerked by the strike of a fish. The weight was then free to run

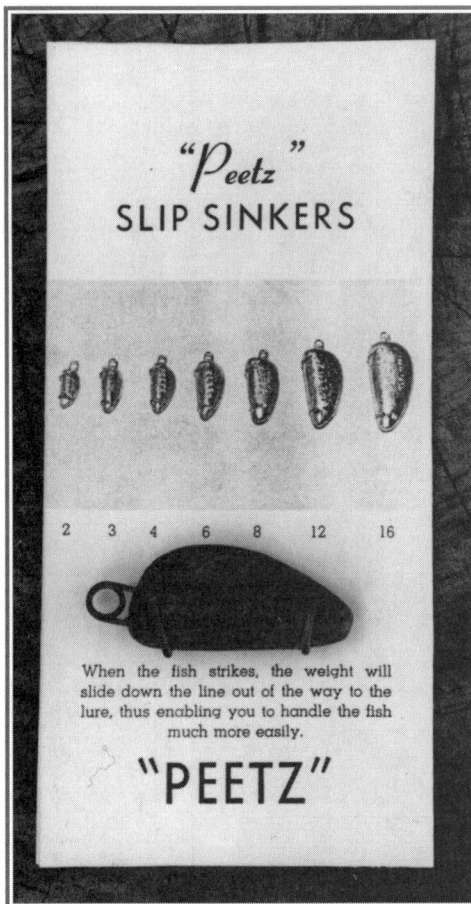

Fig. 6.6 A big item in Peetz sales: early patented lead weights.

down to a swivel that was close enough to the lure to permit the fish to be wound in to within a rod length of the top line guide. Once the patent expired, the idea was taken up by several West Coast manufacturers. The Peetz series was produced in 2-, 3-, 4-, 6-, 8-, 12-, and 16-ounce weights. Despite the advent of downriggers, the sliding weight is still a popular item of the Peetz company.

The immediate postwar period was a period of opportunity for the new family business. People had returned to saner occupations, with time to attend to important matters like fishing. A huge influx of immigrants was underway. And of particular significance, the flow of popular wooden reels from Britain was rapidly drying up. The great names of Hardy, Allcock, Milward, and others had turned almost wholly to metal construction, no doubt aided by a huge pool of machinery and machinists to draw upon after the war. Other companies, such as Heaton, whose reels had previously found their way to the West Coast, had simply disappeared or dropped tackle manufacture altogether.

New businesses appeared and former businesses reappeared in Victoria, Sooke, and Sidney. Several local entrepreneurs saw opportunities emerging with the growth of fishing. Among them was Nick Lupkoski. For some years he worked from his home in Victoria, and his 6-inch reel became quite well known locally. Later in life he moved to Sidney, where he farmed strawberries. Eventually he resumed production of his reels, in three sizes, 4-, 5-, and 6-inch (Fig. 6.7).

Fig. 6.7   Like Peetz, Lupkoski made reels in 4-, 5-, and 6-inch diameters.

A robust brass and mahogany Nottingham, the Lupkoski reel is sometimes confused with the Peetz (Fig. 6.8). Although superficially similar, its construction is different in almost every detail. The Lupkoski has a striking strap. In addition to a straight component, reaching across the back-plate, the strap has a heavy ring of brass reinforcing the underlying wood. In contrast to Peetz reels, the entire strap and foot were cast as a unit. Later models are stamped with the words "MADE BY N. LUPKOSKI SIDNEY B.C."; earlier models display their Victoria origin. Vancouver Island Brass Foundry of Victoria supplied the castings.

The 6-inch reel had particularly large handles, 1¼ inches in diameter. They were set in flat handle-plates, similar to those of early Peetz design. The interior was quite distinct; partly lined with brass, it contained a check actuated by a sliding plate and held in the grip of an almost perfectly circular spring. The spindle was a massive ⅝-inch in diameter; its distal end was threaded, presumably to hold grease.

Some have suggested that Lupkoski followed the Peetz design, but clearly he did not. Nick Lupkoski simply adapted the basic Nottingham pattern to his idea of a rugged trolling reel. Other than having reels in three sizes, there is only one point of similarity: he too used a four-

Fig. 6.8. This 6-inch Lupkoski reel (left) made in the 1980s might be mistaken for a much older Peetz reel (right).

piece drag assembly, comprising a fiber washer, a domed brass D-washer, a wing nut and lock screw. It is true that, during the earlier years of production, he visited the Peetz factory to buy parts for his reels, but later models show little or no indication of this. Even less supportable is the notion that Boris Peetz copied Lupkoski's reel. Quite apart from fundamental differences in construction, there is abundant evidence of Boris's much earlier beginnings.

Many of Lupkoski's reels were sold privately. He did not approach the production levels of the Peetz factory. Nevertheless, there were some sales through Robinson's Sporting Goods in Victoria. There was a lull of at least a decade in which no reels were produced, but Lupkoski resumed production after moving near Sidney, and continued to produce reels in small numbers until his death in 1988.

Lupkoski's efforts notwithstanding, and for at least a few years, Peetz and Son remained in the enviable position of having few competitors in a rapidly expanding marketplace.

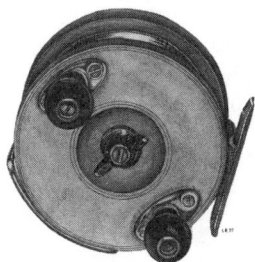

CHAPTER 7

Brentwood Gear

The Victoria-Saanich Inlet Anglers' Association had a prominent place in the affairs of many Victorians. It was a huge organization, with a membership of well over 2000 in some years. Businesses donated substantial prizes for the huge fishing derbies; some, such as Woodwards, Household Finance, and Robinson's Sporting Goods, established trophies in their own names. Boris Peetz had been among the first to do so, with the Hookum Trophy for the biggest fish weighed in by a Junior member of the Association. The fate of the Hookum Trophy is uncertain, for it is not mentioned in postwar yearbooks. However, an individual Peetz Cup (see Fig 5.3) was awarded to then Junior member Bobby Redgrave in 1937. The Peetz Cup may have originated as the Hookum Trophy; I could not locate it.

Boris also donated the Chinook Club Peetz Annual Trophy, now with the secretary of the remnant Association, Stephen Rose. The Chinook Cup was awarded for the largest salmon caught by a new member of the Chinook Club. It was won in 1952 by J.R. James with a 49-pound fish (see Fig. 5.5), which remained unbeaten for twenty-five years until Bill Bell caught a fish of 51 pounds 10 ounces. By then, a fish over 40 pounds was quite exceptional in the Inlet. Most fish were caught on what had come to be known as "Brentwood gear."

Although I had fished the Saanich Inlet many times, I had never tried "Brentwood gear." Most of my fishing had been done with a long, limber rod and light line designed for mooching. Clearly, any author of a book about Peetz reels is obligated to try them out in the same manner Boris and his friends had fished in the halcyon years of the Inlet. I would need guidance. Ivan and Judy Peetz directed me to one man in particular: John Rose.

According to Ivan and Judy, John had fished with their father soon after arriving in Victoria from England in 1952. Here was an opportunity

Fig. 7.1. John Rose, aboard Salar, *adjusts the drag on his Recorder.*

to get more insight into the man behind the name, as well as to learn how he fished. "Do you want to go fishing?" was the reply when I introduced myself over the phone. John had a familiar accent, decidedly London.

John Rose lives to fish, and he still keeps his beloved 26-foot double-ender at Brentwood. But at eighty-two, he no longer drives, and seizes any opportunity to get a lift from his apartment in Victoria. So it was that I found myself aboard the *Salar* on a fairly brisk April morning, twenty years almost to the day since I boated my unforgettable first chinook in the Saanich Inlet. We soon found common ground. John grew up in Croydon, I in Wimbledon, just a few miles away. I would not learn much about Boris Peetz, but I was about to get a lesson in the use of "Brentwood gear" and an earful on the decline of the Inlet .

The *Salar* is an angler's boat. There are few signs of its earlier life as a navy cutter. A partly covered rear deck provides protection from wind and rain. Its warm cabin is thickly painted, with very little brightwork to polish and no fancy teak to varnish. Over the windows hang dozens of hooks adorned with spoons, hootchies, and herring teasers.

The big two-cylinder Volvo diesel thumped amidships as we pulled out of the marina and headed north towards Deep Cove. John tended to the engine as gently as he would a child, adjusting its pace to a slow and reassuring beat. We passed between Seanus Island and Henderson Point, and I reminded myself that we were close to the summer cottage where William Hall and Boris had ventured forth with handlines almost eighty years earlier.

I had taken the wheel as soon as we cleared the dock. John prepared his tackle. We would be fishing with 8-foot fiberglass trolling rods made by Peetz, each equipped with a 6-inch Recorder filled with Monel wire line. This was to be a day in the traditional Brentwood style, although John didn't see it that way. He simply prefers to fish with such gear, for it gives him a very direct feel of the fish while it is being played. He made an important observation, one that I was to hear again from a household name in Campbell River, Joe Painter. It takes more skill to land a salmon on wire line than on nylon line. Many fish are lost at the initial impact of a strike because of the inability of wire to absorb shock.

Modern rods offer a similar advantage. The now-common 10-foot mooching rod, fitted with a light reel and nylon monofilament, is altogether softer and more forgiving, although it must be used with a downrigger if any depth is to be reached. It all adds up to more intense pressure on the salmon resource.

The mooching rod is quite unsuitable for another device, the planer. The planer is similar to a kite. But instead of soaring upwards against the wind, a planer dives down beneath the boat, against the pressure of water. No weight is required, but the device must be tripped before it can be retrieved, otherwise it will put great strain on angler and tackle. One of the requirements of a planer is a strong and stiff rod. The rod must be able to handle the not-inconsiderable pressure developed by a planer as it dives to fishing depths; it must also be capable of tripping the planer when needed, a feat quite impossible with a soft rod. A hooked fish will trip a planer automatically, and it can then be played without the drag of a pound or more of lead on the line. Nevertheless, the planer is not without its own special effect on a fast-moving fish, as it tries to plow the water in a different direction.

Bill Thorne, who in the 1930s ran a small tea shop that catered to Brentwood anglers, is credited with development of the sliding-weight planer. A movable weight on the wire keel of the planer can be set to control the depth and length of line to be fished. Eventually rights to the sliding-weight planer were passed to Gerry MacPherson, another Victoria innovator. Gerry developed the "Can-Adapter" that allowed direct connection of an ordinary fuel-can to an outboard motor. In his view, the planer was an integral part of deep-water "Brentwood gear" and contributed to the success of the Peetz Recorder. Tom Moss, who for many years has manufactured salmon plugs and spoons at his shop in Sooke, sees the advent of stiff fiberglass rods as a critical development in deep-water fishing. A convergence of ideas suddenly opened up new possibilities for anglers—in this case, deep-water trolling.

John Rose clipped a pink planer on each rod. He had a few feet of dacron leader at the end of the Monel for ease of handling. Then he fastened a herring teaser on the end of about forty feet of monofilament behind the planer. With practised fingers, he sliced off two long tapered strips from a frozen herring and rigged each of the teasers. The first rig was lowered into the water, and John watched intently as the strip rolled and shimmered in the early morning light.

Satisfied, he paid out some line (Fig. 7.1). The rod jerked downwards as the planer bit into its descent. With the rod now in its holder, John asked me to let the reel unwind slowly. "A hundred feet," I called. John answered with "More." "One fifty." Again the reply, "More." I decided to just let it run until John told me to stop. "How much now?" he asked after a while. "Two hundred and eighty feet," I announced, expecting a reprimand. "Give it another twenty and that will do," and there it sat. We set the second rod with 200 feet of line. Judging from the steep angle at which the Monel cut the water, the first rod was fishing far deeper than I had ever fished before, even with a downrigger, and the second rod was fishing at well over 150 feet.

We sat back and poured hot coffee from our vacuum flasks. Just the sight of the steaming cups warmed our spirits in the chilly air. Talk turned to days gone by. John did not wish to reminisce about the early fifties. In fact he was quite reticent about Boris, the Victoria-Saanich Inlet Anglers' Association, and other local history I was keen to hear of. His memory clarified as he cast further back, and locked in on the early forties and his exploits in the British navy during World War II. He spoke of frigates he had served on, of enemy planes shot down, and of submarines sunk. Later in the day it would all come back when I returned John to his small apartment—a veritable museum of war in the North Atlantic.

The talk of action was in sharp contrast to our fishing success. The sun came up and warmed the air a trifle. We had started out in a flat calm. Wood smoke hung in the treetops of Willis Point. The high hills above Bamberton lay mirrored along the Inlet. But as we turned into Pat Bay we sensed a change. The wind had picked up. Despite its shelter, the Inlet can be whipped into whitecaps without much warning.

As the Institute of Ocean Sciences came into view the portside rod dipped slightly, and then again. With deliberation, John lifted the rod: there was a fish on but the planer had not tripped. He passed me the rod and told me to trip it. My performance did not impress him. Grabbing the rod back, he smartly lowered the tip to the water and jerked it back with all his might. Too late, our fish had gone. I felt like a Navy recruit getting my first tongue-lashing, although this one was silent. John rebaited the teaser and I turned the *Salar* in a wide arc, beginning our return. Almost immediately the second rod started to rattle in its holder. This time John tripped the planer and reeled in without my help. Two hundred feet of line later, a foot-long salmon, or shaker, appeared alongside. John lent over the gunwale, grabbed the single hook with pliers, and shook the young fish free.

We fished past Dyer Rocks and Coles Bay without incident. We had had a good trip, considering the depleted state of Saanich Inlet. But John Rose wanted fish, and if he could not have salmon he would try for other delicacies. The wind had died down. In a spot I pledged to secrecy, John slid the engine into neutral. The big diesel beat slowly on the edge of stall. He rigged two light rods with something I had not seen since leaving England—paternosters. The 10-inch spreaders had been made up locally in stainless-steel wire. With a 2-ounce weight at the end and hooks dangling from its spreaders, each hung like a tiny artificial tree. We chopped the remaining herring scraps into small pieces and lowered the baited paternosters to the bottom. Straight away we got bites, and, to my surprise, I hauled in three pan-size flounders. In a few minutes we had enough for a good meal.

John lamented the paucity of our catch. It is not just the salmon that have left the Inlet. The ground fish too have gone. Lingcod are virtually a thing of the past, and rock cod, once left in peace in favor of salmon, are scarce. Now he even has to protect the whereabouts of his sole hole. As we cleaned our mess of fish, John and I debated whether catch-and-release made sense, for doubt surrounds the survival of released fish. We agreed that salmon are cheaper to buy in the supermarket than to catch on the high seas. A government study on the economic value of British Columbia's salmon found that the average rod-caught chinook or coho in 1994 cost the angler $671. Even then, they are a

Fig. 7.2. Brentwood fact: bronze button and certificate awarded to Victoria-Saanich Inlet Anglers' Association member Bill Hoskyn for a chinook of 24½ pounds taken on Brentwood gear August 1, 1946.

bargain by European standards: in 1997, *Trout and Salmon* magazine quoted current values at £6000 per fish on good rivers. No wonder we sometimes have to sneak out to wet a line.

As it turned out, 1996 was the year that anglers did release a large number of salmon. When the federal Department of Fisheries and Oceans banned retention of chinooks in northern and western waters, operators of fishing lodges had few options. It would have to be catch-and-release for their main drawing card. Revenues and jobs in the industry were hit hard. But the ban was accepted philosophically by a surprisingly large number of anglers, many of whom traveled great distances to fish the fabled waters of the Queen Charlotte Islands and the west side of Vancouver Island.

The current demise of the West Coast fishery is a topic of intense debate among interested parties. Many factors are at play. Some are easily identified, although none are fully understood. Commercial, traditional, and recreational interests vie for fish that are already beset with unrelenting loss of breeding habitat. Some fish appear to have changed their migration routes. Large numbers of coho show up on the west side of Vancouver Island, leaving the valuable recreational fishery of the

Fig. 7.3. Brentwood fantasy: a 24-pound chinook, a No. 7 Chinook spoon, and a modern rod and 5-inch reel by Peetz.

Strait of Georgia impoverished. Perhaps most serious of all, an increasing frequency of El Niño currents has led to devastating predation from warm-water mackerel.

John Rose does not get philosophical about his fishing or the fish. To him, the act of fishing is what he enjoys. The catch is important but not critically so, although it has become so for others. Ivan, Betty, and Judy Peetz have fished the ritual Cowichan Bay "Snob Derby" for decades, in celebration of the once-magnificent coho. In 1995, Ivan did relatively well. He caught two of the top three fish brought in that day. Unfortunately they were the only fish caught. To declare the results of the 1996 derby disappointing would be an understatement. Not a single fish was caught.

Fundamentally, we have to change our attitude. Our passion for fishing must include a reverence for fish. The balance of means and end is important in angling. Perhaps technology has diminished the essence of angling, although those who have the toys appear to enjoy them. John Rose has fished with simple "Brentwood gear" for over forty years, has loved every minute of it, and has caught his share of salmon. He will not change now, nor does he need too. No amount of sophisticated equipment will improve his catch in Saanich Inlet. If the Saanich Inlet is a portent of things to come for the West Coast, there will be many more than John Rose lamenting.

CHAPTER 8

New Challenges

Writing in the Victoria *Times Colonist* in 1985, Ernie Fedoruk referred to Peetz reels as "Canadian classics." The word "classic" is a fitting description for Boris's wood and brass creations. The wood he selected was mahogany. It was a good choice and would serve his enterprise well. Warm to the hand and lustrous to the eye, mahogany glows with an indefinable depth of color that varies from rich amber to deep ruby red. Small wonder that it has been a favorite with generations of furniture-makers. Oddly, mahogany is not noted for durability. It must be seasoned thoroughly before it is worked because it has a tendency to split as it dries. But its deep interlocking grain turns well, accepts drilling and fasteners, and with the right finish remains tough and stable.

The true mahoganies come from a family of African trees, *Meliaceae*. These days, almost any reddish tropical hardwood is liable to be sold as "mahogany." Much of what is now marketed in North America is red luan, comprising species of *Shorea* originating in Southeast Asia; it is also grown in Central America. Such academic trivia would have been of little interest to Boris Peetz as he scoured Victoria's dockyard for suitable pieces of dunnage. As production grew he began to purchase timber from hardwood importers.

From time to time, Boris had difficulty in obtaining mahogany, and tried other species. Early models were turned from nondescript woods. Later variants can be found in walnut, maple, oak, and imported species such as jarrah from Australia. When Japanese timber agencies captured the world market for a number of tropical hardwoods, Boris turned to a Hawaiian species, koa, noted for its beauty in traditional furniture and wood carving. Unfortunately, *Acacia koa* had not been tested under the rigorous conditions of salmon fishing, and many of the reels split after a few months of use. The supply of tropical hardwoods has become a conservation issue of global proportions but has not affected the company in recent years; most of the wood used today is Honduran mahogany, from plantations in Belize.

No matter how carefully the wood is selected, subtle variations remain in color and grain, so that each piece is unique. But the individuality of each reel does not stop there. From the beginning, Peetz reels were constructed almost entirely from handmade components. According to Bill Hooson, the only parts that are truly interchangeable are the fiber washers, check pawl, reel foot, and line guard. Nevertheless, any model of Peetz reel is repairable.

Peetz reels emerged from the war more or less unchanged in materials and design. But a new synthetic material was now making waves through many industries, and nowhere would the impact be greater than in fishing tackle manufacture. The material was nylon. It offered the strength of steel, but was limp and colorless. It could be produced in unlimited lengths in uniform diameters and breaking strengths. According to Harlan Major, nylon was first used by freshwater fishermen in leaders of braided fibers. But monofilament quickly asserted itself as the pre-eminent line for many types of fishing, both freshwater and saltwater.

Among nylon's characteristics is its propensity for elastic stretch. In this it differs markedly from metal lines, and while linen cuttyhunk also stretched, it did so to a much lesser degree. Elasticity presented a new and serious problem to many fishing reels on which it was used. Stretch, developed under the tension of winding in heavy weights or fish, translates into forces of compression on the reel's drum. The compression builds up with each turn of the reel, sometimes with catastrophic results.

When I first moved to Victoria in 1978 I brought a 6-inch Pflueger Sal-trout reel that had been used with a light wire line for lake trout in Ontario. Within a week I was on the water, in the still-productive Saanich Inlet, with my Pflueger loaded with 750 feet of new 30-pound nylon line. My kind host for the day was Doug Taylor, a colleague from work. By one of those curious coincidences in life, Doug's wife Wendy happened to be Ola Peetz's daughter, although I was unaware of the relationship at the time.

As soon as my planer touched the water, it began its deep and wobbling dive into the fiord. After a while, I wound in to check the lure, in the process failing to release the unfamiliar planer, and thus hauling against some resistance. All was fine, until I let out the planer again. Doug's face split, first in a grin, then into a fit of uncontrollable mirth, as bits of line fell into the water and boat. The line had become so compressed after a single retrieve that it forced its way through numerous perforations in the metal drum of the reel, severing itself repeatedly in the process. A slow learner, I would repeat the error later in the year, with rather tragic results.

Most trolling reels are not perforated, and something other than the line has to give. Nylon line was the demise of many good trolling reels, whether of wood, metal, or Bakelite. On some, the outer face of the drum would yield; on others, the brass plate would distort, jamming the reel. Peetz reels were no exception, although their robust construction held up better than many imported counterparts. Often the damage could be repaired, and the company will still rebuild its reels, and those of other makers, for a modest sum.

Even today, Peetz reels can be found packed with nylon monofilament. Such reels almost invariably show evidence of such treatment in the core of the drum, whose grain is compressible. The core takes on a slightly oval cross-section, with its longer axis parallel to the wood grain. The core diameter may thus vary by as much as 9/16 inch, although the distortion is usually much less.

The arrival of nylon led to another weakness in design. As cuttyhunk became obsolete, the capacity of the drum could be reduced. The modified reels, which include most of those produced after the war, have narrower and shallower drums. The wing nut for drag control is neatly recessed into the face of the drum; the recess reduces the thickness of wood left near the core and can result in failure at this point. Eventually, the compression problem with monofilament nylon would be avoided with the use of braided nylon, which had less stretch, and this proved to be a popular solution.

Nottingham happens to be the birthplace of my grandfather, John William Selby, as well as the reel by its name. He encouraged my tentative forays into fishing by giving me

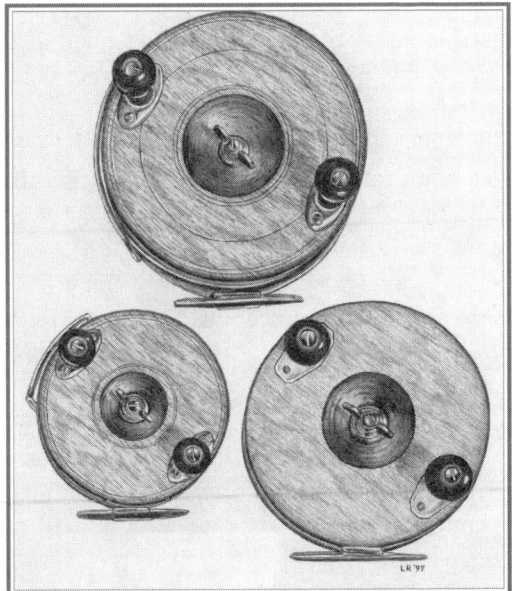

the tackle he had used in his youth. There was a poacher's rod in perhaps eight sections of greenheart, a leather wallet containing long needles for threading hooks through dead baits, and, of course, a wooden reel. The 3½-inch Nottingham was the only piece to come to Canada with me, and remained unused until I ventured out bucktailing in Deep Cove at the north end of Saanich Inlet. That was in the late 1970s, when magnificent coho entered the Inlet each fall.

Not fully equipped for the tremendous variety of fishing I now had on my doorstep, I rigged up a stiff spinning rod with my grandfather's reel for our first morning out. Just after dawn, a large fish hit my Gray Ghost in the bubbling wake of our boat. After several hard runs, the salmon came to the net. It turned the scales at nine pounds. But as I prepared to let line out I discovered success came with a price. The little reel was exploding in slow motion, its drum-plates bulging and splitting. It had been packed with monofilament nylon, and the prolonged tension during the fight had been enough to build up the devastating pressure. I don't think it would have bothered my grandfather, for it fell in splendid action. But I would trade my most valuable Hardy to get that little reel back.

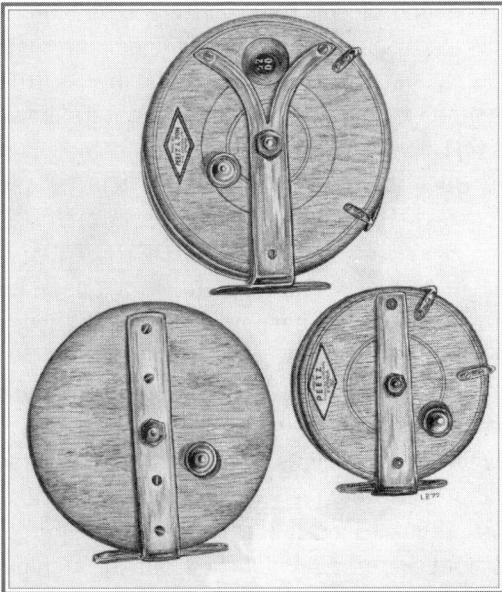

Fig. 8.1. The two sides of classic Peetz reels, captured by the pencil of Loucas Raptis.

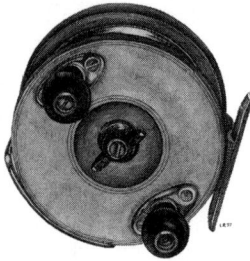

CHAPTER 9

The Next Generation

Boris Peetz died on January 12, 1954. He was in his seventy-first year. For almost half a century, he and his family had built fishing tackle renowned up and down the West Coast. From California to Alaska, Peetz tackle had established a reputation for ruggedness and durability. Maintaining the integrity of Boris's concepts of design and materials was a given, but it would not be without challenge.

Edna inherited the company and left it to Ivan, Judy, and Bud to nurture what had become a legacy for the West Coast salmon angler. As might be expected, all of the Peetz children grew up with a love of the sea, and to this day are keen boaters. Judy and Ivan, in particular, had inherited their father's enthusiasm for fishing.

The approach of the new generation was to be conservative. Significantly, the company title, Peetz and Son, remained unchanged. The Peetz line of tackle was still popular, and the business was favored with a steadily growing population along the coast, many of whom were drawn to the fabulous salmon fishing. But the costs of materials and labor were also growing. Emphasis would be put on improving efficiency, and on refining the production process. The products themselves would stay the course charted by Boris.

Small changes appeared in the reels. Ivan developed a talent for producing dies. Handle-plates, which had been hand-cut and shaped from sheet brass, were the first components to be punched out in a "one-shot" operation. Ivan's machines increased productivity by as much as fifty times that of the equivalent hand operation. The strap and foot assembly, hand cut and beveled from heavy sheet brass, and soldered and riveted to form the backbone of every reel, was especially laborious and expensive to produce. In 1959, a large punch press was acquired, and by 1960 the strap and foot were being punched out as a single piece, a process that has proved satisfactory ever since. In 1958, the check button, previously penetrated by the actuating screw, was now soldered inside so that the screw no longer appeared on the outside.

The line guard of the reel maintained a peculiarity. Not that its design is unusual, for the simple wire Bickerdyke had been the standard for countless Nottinghams of the past. Could it be that all North American anglers are left-handed? Hardly, but the fact remains that reels from this side of the Atlantic are almost invariably made with handles on the right, yet most anglers hold their rods with that hand, until they start to operate the reel. With one exception, every Peetz reel I have seen was set up thus, with the line guard positioned accordingly; the only exception is a 6-inch pre-war reel in my collection that never had a line guard fitted. About half of the imported Nottinghams I have seen were set up for reeling with the left hand.

There was a need to improve fabrication of the brass back-plate of the drum. Traditionally it had been marked out with dividers, and cut with tin snips before being spun to shape on a lathe. The final cut was always a hazardous procedure, as the curled trimmings could suddenly fly off from the plate like razor-sharp shrapnel. Now the piece could be pressed out in one operation.

Judy had developed her skills long before becoming a partner with her brothers. She had polished Hookum spoons and varnished Recorder reels by the thousand. Judy's modesty belies the part she played in the company's success. Countless salmon have been taken on inexpensive cane rods fashioned by her hands. Peetz and Son never built split-cane rods, but fiberglass rods were a different matter. A line of five rods, from light to moderately heavy, was developed to meet various needs for salmon trolling. Some were fitted with the patented roller guides and pulley tips that Boris developed. The company was open to custom orders, a practice that continues to this day. Weights and lures, swivels and flashers all contributed to the healthy output from the increasingly cramped factory on Johnson Street.

All the family fished and sailed, and they also became interested in skiing. Bud and like-minded enthusiasts formed the Snowbird Ski Club and developed skiing facilities at Mount Brenton, and later at Green Mountain, on Vancouver Island. Ultimately their efforts would be thwarted by acts of vandalism. By then Peetz and Son had ventured into selling and renting ski equipment (Fig. 9.1). Many years later they would sell the enlarged retail business to Jeune Bros, the venerable tent and flag company next door. The two companies would carry on, side by side at 570 and 574 Johnson Street, until 1973, when more space became imperative. (Years earlier, Ivan had knocked down the wall between 572

Fig. 9.1. Advertisement in the 1963 Victoria-Saanich Inlet Anglers' Association Year book at the height of Peetz tackle and ski business.

and 574 (Fig. 9.2), causing the address 572 Johnson Street to disappear.)

Bud had left the company in 1958 and moved to Scotty Plastics, now a well-established manufacturer of fishing accessories in Victoria. Among other things, he produced designs and tooling for Scotty's first rod holder. In 1957, Scotty Plastics had begun supplying plastic indicator discs for Peetz Recorder reels, the hand-punched aluminum discs having become too expensive to produce.

Scotty Plastics are probably best known for their downriggers, the advent of which might have spelled serious trouble for Peetz, whose focus was on trolling equipment. Downriggers did away with line weights, which enabled the fisherman to use light lines, light rods, and smaller reels; they also had depth indicators built in, which would seem to obviate the importance of the Recorder reel.

Anglers did not abandon their Peetz reels. Indeed, many welcomed the opportunity to use the traditional reel without heavy weights, for the problem with nylon line was now much reduced. Besides, there were still lots of pink and coho salmon to be had around Victoria and Vancouver Island, and these could be taken at depths requiring only a few ounces of lead weight, or even on the surface. Some would argue that downriggers were best avoided if possible. Mooching with little or no added weight, even at depths in excess of 100 feet, was also gaining in popularity.

But if the downrigger threat could be stemmed, there were other challenges to confront. Penn, Ocean City and other U.S. makers were inundating the North American market with inexpensive multipliers that already had an established following. The phenolic plastic, Bakelite, had proved itself as a tough material capable of withstanding saltwater use, and large numbers of reels in the 4- to 5-inch class appeared under such names as Allcock (notably the Aerialite, in two sizes), Elo and Paramount from Britain, and Steelite and Alvey from Australia. In just a few

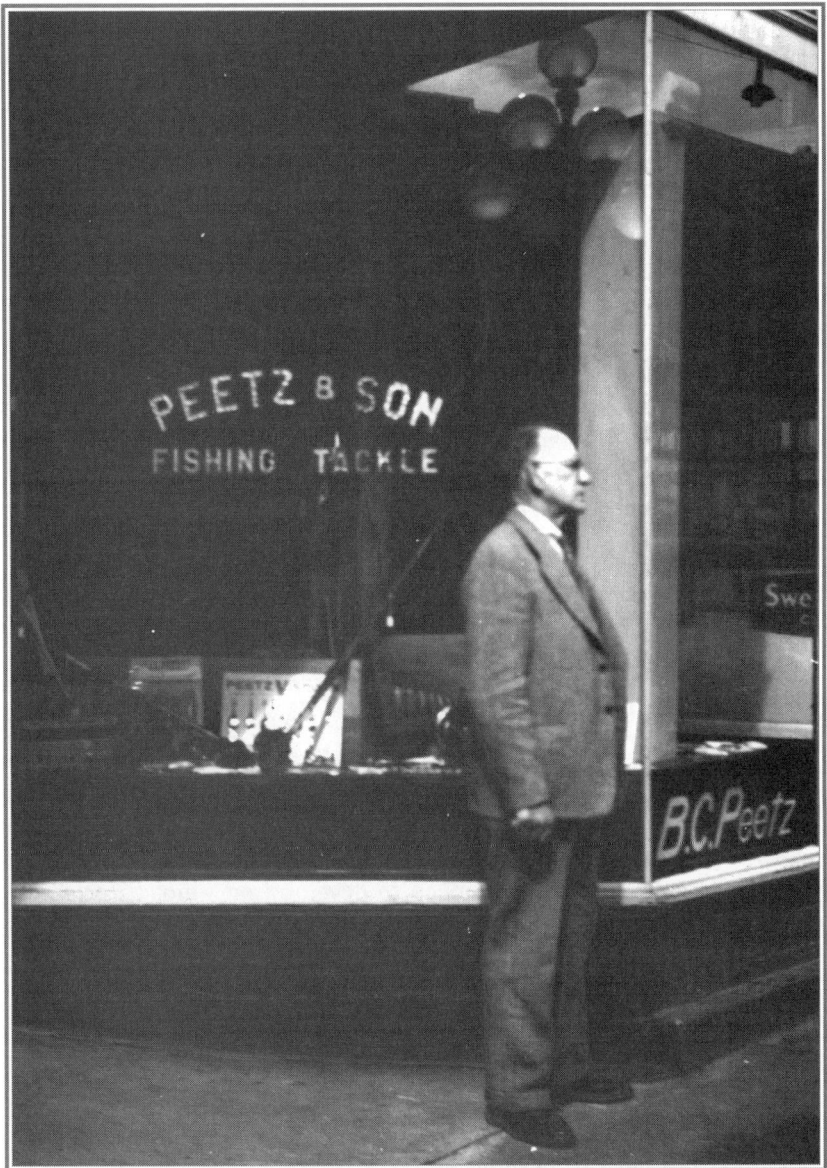

Fig. 9.2. Boris Peetz at the shop, 574 Johnson Street, 1940s.

years almost all of these would disappear, to be replaced by unfamiliar names from Asia, such as Daiwa and Shimano, and a transplanted Mitchell. The great influx from Asia had yet to materialize, but it is no small wonder that the locally made mahogany and brass classics managed to weather such onslaught in their traditional territory.

The company changed its name in 1967. The new title soon appeared in the familiar diamond-shaped labels on their reels, "Made by Peetz Tackle Ltd. 574 Johnson St., Victoria, B.C. Canada." The gold label was now bordered in red, instead of black and red, a point of detail that can help to date specimens with damaged labels.

In the midst of what was a most hectic period for the company, Ivan and Judy decided that the Johnson Street factory could no longer accommodate them. In 1973 they moved their base from downtown Victoria to a small property on Rock Bay Avenue, about a mile away, in a light-industrial sector of town. In the process of moving, the family split off the retail arm of the company. Advertisements in the angler's association yearbook documented the transition (Fig. 9.3) Retail sales would continue for many years under the name "Jeune Bros and Peetz Tackle and Ski" at 570 Johnson Street (Fig. 9.4). Eventually Jeune Bros would drop fishing tackle from their line of sales, along with the Peetz name in the company's title.

The Peetz product line of reels, rods, and other tackle remained more or less unchanged for the next three years. Reels were offered in nominal sizes of 4-, 5-, and 6-inch diameters (in fact they were 3¾, 4¾, and 5¾ inches respectively), with the Recorder still available in the two larger sizes, although the 5-inch was uncommon. The gold and red reel label now sported a new name. It read, " Made by Peetz Manufacturing Ltd. Victoria, B.C." Oddly, the company was listed in the 1973 Victoria Directory as Peetz Tackle Manufacturing Ltd., but this may have been a misprint. No labels with this title have been found.

Intense competition continued to develop from abroad. Incredibly, as it seems in retrospect, Ivan Peetz launched a new reel of the classic Peetz mold into the volatile marketplace (Fig. 8.2). It was a refinement of the 5-inch (nominal) reel, although at 5¼ inches it was ½ inch larger. The drum was narrower and shallower to reduce the amount of nylon line that could be loaded.

We might speculate that the 5¼-inch reel was intended for bucktailing. But two features indicate that Ivan had wider uses in mind. Again with a view to lowering the risk posed by stretched line, heavy cranking was discouraged by the handles being set closer to the spindle and fitted with small knobs. But the clincher was the Recorder feature, calibrated for 25-pound monofilament. Lightness was achieved with a thinner mahogany back-plate, reinforced with glued-in sheet brass that filled the entire inside face. The laminated back-plate was still too thin to accept screws, however, and the standard line guard had to be riveted in place. Because of the reel's unconventional size, the brass strap had

Visit OMAR

Jeune Bros.

OUTDOOR STORE

570 JOHNSON STREET

Island's Largest Sales and Rentals of Camp Equipment

CANVAS TARPS & AWNINGS

Rain Wear and Outdoor Clothing, Etc.

Established 1886

FACTORY 385-7751   RETAIL 384-4322

In Nanaimo, 620 Comox   254-5511

PEETZ TACKLE & SKIS

RETAIL AND REPAIR SERVICE

574 Johnson   **VICTORIA**   383-3652

SPORTS TROLLING RODS and TACKLE

PEETZ RECORDING REELS

Hardwood Reels, Slip Sinkers, "Hookum" Spoons, Extension Handles, Roller Guides, Pulley Tips for wire line fishing, and Water Skis.

COMPLETE SKI & TENNIS SHOP

RETAIL, RENTAL AND REPAIR

Fig. 9.3. Peetz and Jeune Bros advertised separate businesses in the 1978 Year Book, but Peetz had already sold their retail arm.

JEUNE BROS & PEETZ TACKLE & SKI LTD.

570 Johnson Street

Sales & Rentals of camping equipment, canvas tarps, awnings, rain wear, outdoor clothing

Complete Ski & Tennis Shop
Retail & Repair Service

Peetz Rod, Reels & Fishing Tackle

Factory 385-7751   Retail 386-8778

Fig. 9.4. The 1979 Year Book was a year or two behind the news: Jeune Bros absorbed Peetz Tackle and Skis in 1977.

to be machined down from a pressing for the 6-inch. The check and Recorder mechanisms were secured to the back-plate with machine screws, so that the outside had the unusual feature of having screw heads set directly in wood.

The new reel was quickly bought up by local anglers, and few of the original three to four hundred produced are to be found today. It was a special reel, both in its design and because it was the last reel to be introduced while the company was owned by the Peetz family. By 1977, Ivan and Judy had reached the difficult decision that it was time to let go. Boris had five granddaughters, but none of them was keen to step into the family business. His legacy would have to pass to someone else, someone outside the family.

Fig. 9.5. The last reel made by the Peetz family: a narrow-drum 5¼-inch Recorder (1976).

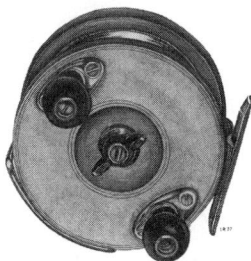

Chapter 10

Changes in the Company

Bill Hooson was no newcomer to the Peetz business. As a young man in the 1950s he worked part-time at the old premises on Johnson Street. He recalls hours of tedious filing, as he shaped and chamfered the brass straps of the big reels. But in 1956 Bill left to seek his fortunes in the retail trade and, later, in the tough business of automotive sales. He spent twelve years with Goodyear Tires. In the long run it was a good move for the company, for Bill learned the rules for survival in an increasingly competitive world. Bill returned to Victoria, with a view to setting up his own business. His timing was fortuitous. After much soul-searching, Ivan and Judy Peetz were eventually convinced by Bill that he could and would preserve the tradition, reputation, and quality of Peetz products. In February 1977 the company was sold to Bill Hooson. There followed a slight change in the reel label, to the Peetz Manufacturing (1977) Company.

The company was about to get some unexpected publicity. In July, 1977, the City of Victoria was visited by HRH Prince Andrew during his tour of northern and western Canada. The Provincial Government laid on a fishing trip, but not in Saanich Inlet. Unfortunately that fishery was already in decline, and a trip to Pedder Bay, west of Victoria, seemed more prudent. Under the watchful eye of outdoor writer Alec Merriman and guided by Peter Gordon, the Prince reeled in his first Pacific salmon on a recently acquired fishing outfit. (Fig. 10.1) He had been presented with a Peetz rod and reel, with accessories provided by other local manufacturers, including plugs and planers. (In a poignant article on the Saanich Inlet, Bruce Obee described how, in earlier days, distinguished visitors had been steered to the Inlet. It was in the Inlet that Jim Gilbert had guided former Canadian Prime Ministers John Diefenbaker and Lester Pearson, former British Columbia Premier W.A.C. Bennett, and Gordie Howe of hocky fame. Jim always used traditional Brentwood gear by Peetz)

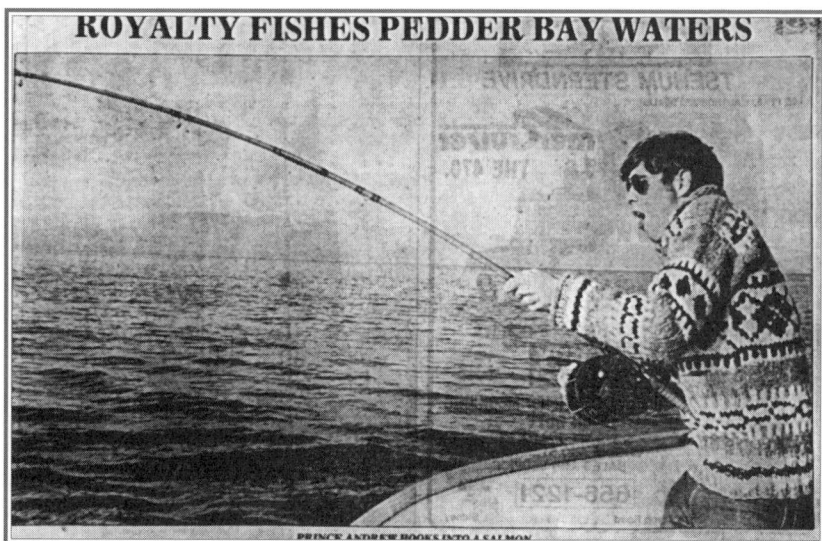

ROYALTY FISHES PEDDER BAY WATERS

PRINCE ANDREW BOOKS INTO A SALMON

Fig. 10.1   One of the famous people to land a salmon on Peetz tackle, Prince Andrew plays his on a big Recorder.

Bill got off to a good start, employing the lessons he had learned elsewhere. He instigated a series of reel clinics; at major fishing centers on Vancouver Island, including Victoria, Nanaimo, Port Alberni, and Campbell River, and continued to provide repair and maintenance service for Peetz products. In the first year, he practically doubled sales in reels, with 12,000 going out to buyers in British Columbia, Washington, and Alaska.

Peetz reels had never explored markets beyond the West Coast, with the exception of some minor sales in the British Columbia Interior, where "Brentwood gear" had been used to good effect by anglers trolling for large rainbow trout in Shuswap, Kootenay, and other deep lakes. Farther east, a significant salmon and trout fishery had developed in the Great Lakes, with large fish being caught in deep, open water. It seemed like a natural market for Peetz equipment.

The market in the Great Lakes region proved very difficult to penetrate. The fishery had emerged more or less in step with the arrival of sport-fishing downriggers. Lead line, wire line, and planers had long been part of lake trout fishing in Ontario and the Great Lakes states, but there had never been a serious attempt to introduce the Peetz line of products there. That is, until the 1980s, when a dealer in Minnesota took a liking to Peetz reels and began to promote them with a glowing brochure that featured an exploded diagram of a Recorder (Fig. 10.2), complete with its thirty-one numbered parts, and a five-year unconditional guarantee.

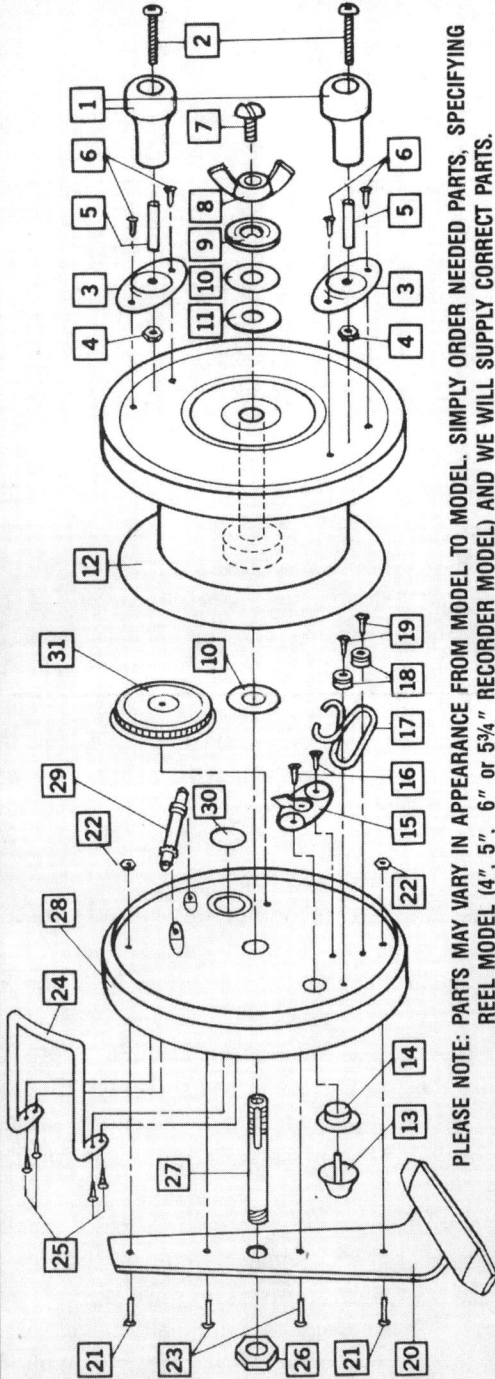

PLEASE NOTE: PARTS MAY VARY IN APPEARANCE FROM MODEL TO MODEL. SIMPLY ORDER NEEDED PARTS, SPECIFYING REEL MODEL (4", 5", 6" or 5¾" RECORDER MODEL) AND WE WILL SUPPLY CORRECT PARTS.

1. Handles
2. Handle Screws
3. Handle Plates
4. Handle Nuts
5. Handle Bushings
6. Handle Plate Screws
7. Spool Retaing Screw
8. Drag Nut

9. Drag Washer
10. Fiber Washers
11. Spring Washer
12. Spool Assembly
13. Clicker
14. Clicker Bushing
15. Clicker Assembly
16. Clicker Screws

17. Clicker Spring
18. Clicker Spring Bushings
19. Clicker Spring Screws
20. Reel Seat
21. Upper & Lower Reel Seat Screws
22. Upper & Lower Reel Seat Nuts
23. Center Reel Seat Screws
24. Line Guide

25. Line Guide Screws
26. Spool Retaining Nut
27. Spool Shaft
28. End Plate Assembly
29. Line Counter Drive Gear *
30. Line Counter Window *
31. Line Counter *
* Recorder Model Only

Fig. 10.2   Exploded diagram of a Peetz reel

While a number of reels were exported east, the demand was not sustained. A promising inquiry from Britain resulted in just a small flurry of sales to that country. Bill Hooson refocused his attention on his traditional customer, the West Coast angler.

But trouble was looming on Canada's West Coast. Concerned over diminishing stocks, the federal fisheries authorities imposed stringent limits on the recreational catch. These were probably more instrumental in reducing the company's sales, by a massive 60 percent in 1980, than the recession that was descending on Canada. British Columbia's economy held up well until late 1981, when it too felt the pangs of recession. The impacts were immediate and lasting on many businesses. In 1979, Bill had twelve full-time staff in the factory on Rock Bay Avenue. When Victoria *Times Colonist* sports writer Ernie Fedoruk met with him in June 1985, Peetz Manufacturing (1977) Company had three full-time employees, including Bill, and a couple of half-time people.

As the Peetz family had requested, Bill Hooson maintained his commitment to tradition. Through ingenuity and determination, he has kept the Peetz name alive and well, deviating very little from the product line for the past twenty years. Regrettably, Ivan's 5¼-inch Recorder had to be dropped from production because of its special requirements in construction. Even the standard reel still entailed over forty separate hand operations in its manufacture. He dropped a few items that had been clearly superseded. But the reels remained more or less unchanged except that, to the consternation of Peetz lovers, he was obliged to shift from wood to plastic handles. In fact, Ivan Peetz had already started to do so, using them on the 5¼-inch Recorder in 1976. The handles and the Recorder disc remain the only parts to be contracted out to suppliers.

It is a minor miracle that the Peetz reel continues to find a place on the shelves of big department stores in Victoria. Unquestionably, it has become impossible for the small company to survive with the original product lines alone, although trolling gear still makes up most of the sales. When Ernie Fedoruk interviewed Bill Hooson in 1985, there were no less than twenty-five different rod styles in the shop rack. But then Bill showed him something that was surely a sign of the times—a handsome putter, its brass and walnut head personalized for some fortunate golfer.

The personal touch was not to be limited to golfers. Reels inscribed for long-service retirees or special events began to appear. In 1990, the company commemorated its own 65th anniversary with appropriately inscribed reels. The reel was in most respects a standard model, except for a few that were turned in camphor wood rather than mahogany, imparting something unique in fishing tackle, a reel that smells. The commemorative reel featured what had now become the company's insignia, a stylish "Peetz" scorched into the face and back-plate; this particular reel also had a wreath with "65 years" emblazoned on the face. At the time, reels still accounted for 30 percent of sales.

Bill Hooson maintains a full line of trolling tackle, including the famous sliding weights, long emulated by other manufacturers after the patent expired. The Hookum lure, going strong in the mid 1980s, has been dropped. But there are several new lures on the scene, lures designed for mooching and shore casting, the latter having made something of a comeback along Victoria's waterfront. On my last visit to the Peetz factory, Bill had just dispatched twenty reels and spare parts to Te Puke in New Zealand. It may be one of many small but untapped markets around the world eager for robust, traditional tackle.

During the summer of 1996 I had occasion to appreciate another addition to the company product line. My friend Mike Bonnor and I were celebrating our recent retirement with a fishing trip to Langara, at the very northern tip of the Queen Charlotte Islands. A few hundred yards off Langara Lighthouse we lucked into a huge halibut. After a not-inconsiderable battle, the fish emerged from the inky depths, just as Damien Grant, chief guide on the MV *Charlotte Princess*, appeared out of nowhere on a Zodiac, bearing hot coffee and other sundries. We were not in the coffee mood. Sizing up our predicament, he clambered aboard our FatCat (an impressively stable platform, and another fishing product from Victoria), and pulled out the vital tool. It was a harpoon, consisting of a short

Fig. 10.3. A Peetz harpoon; simplified boating this 56-pound halibut.

stainless spear mounted on a long shaft of ash, and attached to a stainless steel and nylon lanyard. The shaft of the harpoon bore a reassuring name: Peetz.

Damien immediately secured the lanyard to a cleat on the FatCat. (This was not the best practice, but we had no buoy at the time.) Our young guide made an expert thrust, and the behemoth went berserk. We hauled on the massive head, whose gillplate took the harpoon, and quickly dispatched the fish. It turned the ship's scales at a staggering 262 pounds. Without a shadow of doubt, the fish would not have been boated without the harpoon.

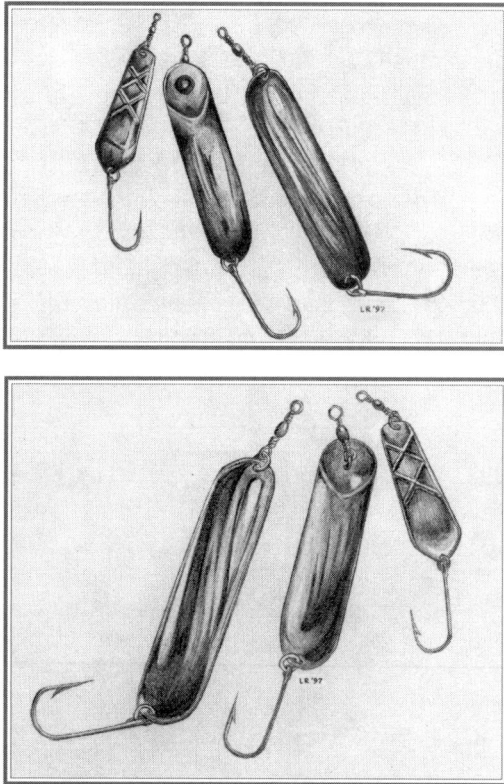

Fig. 10.4. A trio of Peetz spoons: impressions by Loucas Paptis.

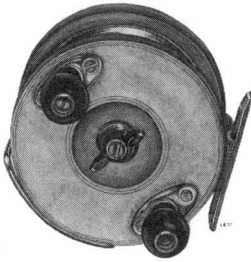

CHAPTER 11

A Reel for the Millennium

The first fishing reels to be made of metal appeared several centuries ago. Nevertheless, wooden reels persisted well into the twentieth century. As we have seen, the Peetz company bore the standard long after almost all others had converted to less organic materials. But it was not until 1995 that the company introduced its first successful all-metal reel, the 5-inch "2000." What is so striking about the reel is the way it is fabricated. Apart from the materials used, it is built the same way Boris Peetz built his wooden Pacifics seventy years earlier (Fig. 11.1).

Fig. 11.1. Evolution of the "2000" maintained construction principles used in wooden reels.

As might be expected, this has not been the company's sole experience with metal reels. But circumstances thwarted the successful introduction of predecessors of the "2000."

In the 1960s, Ivan Peetz designed and built a metal Recorder (Fig. 11.2, 11.3, 11.4). A mere 4¼ inches in diameter, it was the smallest Recorder ever made. Ivan made the reel for his wife, Betty, and she used it for twenty-five years, until the brass plates of the drum began to separate from the plastic core. Discoloration of the metal attests to long

Fig. 11.2. A unique recorder: a 4-inch all-metal Recorder.

Fig. 11.3. Rim gear of the metal Recorder.

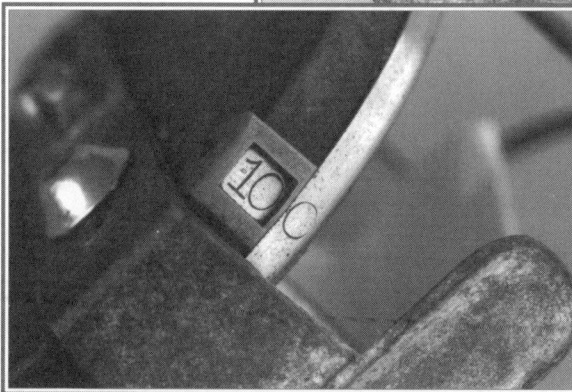

Fig. 11.4. Rim detail of the metal Recorder, indicating 100 feet of line

Fig. 11.5   Unfinished 6-inch all-metal Recorder.

use. An intriguing feature of this unique reel was the line register. The indicator window was conveniently placed on the rim of the back-plate so that it could be seen without having to turn the reel sideways. Numbers on the indicator were stamped onto an annular gear rotating under the rim, actuated by a standard transfer gear. Betty loved to measure the run of a big coho. Ivan started on a second metal Recorder, but the 6-inch reel was never completed (Fig. 11.5).

After purchasing the company, Bill Hooson started thinking about the future of his new enterprise. Of particular concern was the future of the legendary Peetz reel, for numerous modern trolling reels, in steel, alloy, fiberglass, or graphite, were now making inroads on the company's marketplace. He drafted plans for an all-metal reel that would be sufficiently robust to withstand the hard knocks of saltwater fishing. No trolling reel could be guaranteed to withstand the vagaries of nylon line. Nevertheless, the reel would have to perform acceptably with this material since most anglers would use it anyway.

In 1980, a 5-inch all-metal trolling reel bearing the familiar diamond-shaped label appeared in Victoria's tackle dealers. In retrospect, we can see it as the forerunner of the "2000" (Fig. 11.1, 11.6); some of its dimensions were almost identical. Traditional features were also prominent, notably a polished pressed-brass strap fitted to the back-plate with brass screws, the caliper check mechanism, and the time-tested drag assembly of brass wing nut, thrust washer, and lock screw (but with tempered copper and thin fiber washers).

The major innovation lay in the drum, which consisted of two 5-inch brass plates separated by eight brass spacers that formed an open core about 3¼ inches in diameter. Possibly with a view to eventual repairs

Fig. 11.6. Progress in metal reels: coated brass (1980), nickel-plated (1982), and the stainless "2000" (1995).

necessitated by nylon line, the drum was assembled with stainless steel machine screws that passed through the spacers, while a thick brass bushing accepted the spindle. Oddly, while plastic handles had already been adopted for wooden reels, the remaining stock of wood handles were used on the new metal reels. These were set directly on the drum face with slot-head stainless screws. The traditional Bickerdyke line guard, in brass, featured a much-reduced opening of about 1¾ by 1 inches, with an extra cross-member to prevent line from snagging the back-plate; single brass screws secured it to the back-plate.

Unfortunately the 1980 reel had an unexpected flaw. Although the company went to great lengths to procure corrosion-resistant coating from Germany, the treated brass plate did not live up to its promise. After a few months of production it became clear that the new material was prone to corrosion after all. Both back-plate and drum became severely pock-marked after a few excursions on salt water. With the company's reputation at stake, Bill Hooson suspended production and offered to refurbish those sold. The total production run was less than a thousand; curiously, about a hundred of them had a four-digit serial number stamped on the brass strap.

Remedies to the problem were investigated, and about eighteen months later a modified version appeared with nickel-plated components (Fig. 11.1, 11.6). It had two new features: the handles were now larger and of plastic, as used on the 6-inch wooden reel, and the rims of the drum had been rolled over to provide smooth curved surfaces for palming. But corrosion continued to plague the metal. Only a few hundred of these transitional reels were sold before the project was set aside altogether.

It was not a time for risky ventures. The crisis in the salmon fishery, especially in Saanich Inlet, had deepened, and Victoria was getting caught up in a severe recession that was gripping the rest of Canada. Undeterred by setbacks, Bill Hooson still believed that a reliable reel could be made of metal. The company had to move with the times, and offer potential customers a modern counterpart to its traditional pieces. He was encouraged by the performance of the 1980 and transitional models in almost every respect; only the metal finish had let him down.

It would be some years before he was ready to try again, this time with the "2000." He focused on the drum for most of the structural changes, and the result is striking. Bright stainless-steel plates are held against a solid Delrin core by six stainless screws, this time with their slot head hidden under the back-plate. As in the transitional model, the rim of each side is rolled over to provide a smooth edge for palming a fast-moving fish. The "2000" has a plastic grommet under each rim to prevent accumulation of moisture and dirt. Somewhat smaller plastic handles turn on stainless spindles with hexagonal heads, and for the first time in seventy years the traditional drag has gone. The brass wing nut and thrust washer have been replaced by a ribbed plastic knob which overlaps a set of washers. The brass lock screw is retained, but is hidden under a removable plastic cap in the drag's knob.

The rated capacity of the drum is 500 yards of 15-pound-test nylon monofilament, or 300 yards of 30-pound-test; with its spacers set somewhat shallower, the 1980 model had about 20 percent less capacity. The "2000" provides an interesting comparison with the early 6¾-inch Pacific, which was calibrated to hold 300 yards of 60-pound monel. At 22 ounces, it is slightly heavier than the 5-inch mahogany reel.

Flip the "2000" over and the pedigree of this handsome reel is at once apparent (Fig. 11.1). Black enamel only thinly disguises the familiar pressed-brass strap and foot, the Bickerdyke line guard (now back to a large, 3⅛-inch opening, without reinforcement) and the bell-shaped check button. Stainless screws replace brass screws, but their arrangement remains the same. Inside is the now-ancient but reliable caliper check assembly (Fig. 11.7). The most significant concession to progress here is a heavier spindle, some ⅜-inch in diameter, compared to 5⁄16-inch in the 1980 model and all the wooden forerunners.

In general, the assembly of the 2000 has so much in common with its wooden predecessors that one is tempted to ask whether the pursuit of tradition might compromise structural integrity. In fact, the continuity of style was more a matter of economy than of tradition. The basic design had proved itself to be adaptable. Despite a major shift in materials, the "2000" has been designed to incorporate as many existing components as possible. Without such savings in tooling up, it would have been difficult for the small company to venture into a radically new product.

Fig. 11.7. Why fix it? The venerable caliper check in a 5-inch mahogany Standard reel, 1950s, and in the modern "2000".

As its name implies, the 2000 should take the company into the twenty-first century. But once again there are problems ahead. In the year following introduction of the new reel, Fisheries and Oceans decided to impose severe restrictions on chinook salmon. The impact on the West Coast sports fishery was immediate. Saltwater fishing sales dropped by over half. The Sport Fishing Institute of British Columbia estimated that $169 million and 2175 jobs were lost by the industry on the West Coast. The outlook as I write in 1997 is improving slightly. Much to the relief of the sport-fishing industry, a retention limit of four chinook has been restored for northern and western waters in 1997-98. Nevertheless, had Bill Hooson not secured a substantial order of yet another innovation, the outlook in 1996 for Peetz Manufacturing (1977) Ltd. could have threatened the future not only of the "2000" but of the entire company.

Despite the gloomy prospects for salmon fishing, Bill Hooson was smiling when I called in at the Rock Bay shop late in 1995. It was the new "2000" I had come to talk about, but Bill had something else to show me. He had just negotiated a contract to produce 10,000 special 5-inch reels. None would catch fish. He showed me one. The reel had been drilled to accept a quartz clock movement. Handles were set either side of the clock-face, and a modified foot and strap served as the stand. It was finished with a brass line guard and wound with green cord.

Fig. 11.8. The reel for all time may survive setbacks in the fishery, but is time running out for the salmon?

The clock reel (Fig. 11.8) is an attractive novelty and finds an eager clientele, especially in the United States where it was featured in the Orvis and other notable catalogues. Set the alarm, and you are awakened by "Fish on!" and the sound of a screaming reel (a Peetz, of course). By the end of 1996, Bill had sold over 30,000 reel clocks, giving the company the best year in its history. When Carla Wilson put the company on the front page of the *Times Colonist* Business section in March 1997, Peetz Manufacturing had seven full-time and two part-time employees, more than double the number reported by Ernie Fedoruk twelve years earlier.

Bill has gone one step further, with a small clock movement set in a 3½-inch wooden fly reel. He has even produced the fly reel by itself, which can hardly be expected to challenge the staggering choice available to the modern flyfisher, but might just find the special niche that has enabled the Peetz company to survive over seven decades.

Metal reels, reels that tell time, and fly reels made of wood are just a few of the diverse products now coming out of the little factory on Rock Bay Avenue in Victoria, BC. Diversity and innovation are the keys to adapting in a rapidly changing world. The lesson was learned by Boris

Peetz decades earlier with his most famous product—the reel that measures line.

Fig. 11.9. This ancient lathe turns thousands of reels every year.

Fig. 11.10. Some of the discs will reel in fish but many more will house timepieces.

CHAPTER 12

A Painter Worth a Thousand Words

It is a matter of attitude. As long as we regard fish as something to own and exploit, we will strive to maximize our catch in the most expedient manner possible. Unfortunately we lack the insight to do this sustainably—that is, in perpetuity—not just for the next five-year planning horizon. Even when they are managed well, our fisheries have to contend with uncontrolled catches offshore, continuing habitat loss, climatic variability, and possible long-term climatic change. If the latter manifests itself as forecast, a massive commitment will be needed from all of us to safeguard our natural resources through a period of unprecedented upheaval.

We need to question whether we really can manage anadromous fish. In *Home Pool*, a tribute to the Atlantic salmon and people who care for it, Philip Lee draws on the wisdom of Wilfred Carter. Carter, a noted salmon biologist, and first President of the International Atlantic Salmon Foundation, made observations of little comfort to us on this side of the continent:

> *The disappointing thing to me is that, with all of the curtailment of the commercial fishery and the catch-and-release fishery that anglers have been practicing for quite a while, we're not seeing a resurgence of salmon stocks as we expected. I find that very disturbing. But I find it also perplexing because we don't really know why. The ocean doesn't seem to be producing as many salmon now as it used to.*

As the fish become more scarce, or more difficult to catch, anglers look to more effective means for locating and catching them. We are succeeding. Increasing affluence coupled with modern technology have put into our hands incredibly sophisticated instruments for destroying salmon. High-speed boats, sonar, depth sounders, fish finders, downriggers, graphite rods, slipping-clutch reels and ultra-fine elastic lines conspire to ensure further diminution of our resource. The latest gadget, the global positioning system or GPS, enables us to navigate through fog to an unmarked destination with pinpoint accuracy, and return in the dark with our catch.

At times, sport fishing representatives have adopted a holier-than-thou stance, pointing to the relatively small numbers of fish caught, and the high value of each fish added to local, provincial, and national economies. All of which is true, of course. But can anglers do more to conserve the fish they hold in such high esteem? I found an answer in the Salmon Capital of the World.

I went to Campbell River with the intention of exploring links between the Peetz reel and this famous salmon fishery. The Pacific Reel had made its debut in the year the Tyee Club was founded, 1924. By then the venue was well known to the sport fishing world. Anglers from Britain and the United States, in particular, had been gathering there every summer since Sir Richard Musgrave broadcast his catch to the world in *The Field*. They came in greater and greater numbers, and, since little tackle was available locally, brought in many foreign rods and reels. Guides became familiar with the great makes of the time. Some of them became the fortunate owners of high quality tackle, left by departing grateful anglers.

When the Painter family developed a boat rental business they supplied tackle for those who arrived empty handed. For whatever reason, Boris Peetz did not seize the opportunity this presented. Perhaps with a little more promotion in Campbell River he might have established a prestigious market for his tackle. Nevertheless, some of his reels were bought and used by local guides and anglers. Certainly, his sliding weight was a standard part of the locally used gear.

One person who did use Peetz reels by preference was Ross Spires. Ross rowed the famous Tyee Pool for many years, and has several trophies to his credit. In 1981 he took the coveted Dr. Julien E. Benjamin Trophy for the largest number of tyee rowed. Ross almost always used Peetz reels, and had something to say about the 4-inch model. He found the smallest of the Peetz line to be in perfect balance with the light rods he preferred. The smooth wide rim was ideal for palming a running fish. He liked the low maintenance needed. When a drag washer wore out he would cut a replacement out of pork rind. He rowed for Betty Davis when she took the Tyee Man trophy for 1973 with a 57-pound fish; it was one of four tyee that she and her husband Elmer took that year, and all were caught on Peetz reels (Elmer also did well in 1972 and 1974, winning the

Fig. 12.1. Reels from Campbell River: Heard and Wilson "Tyee," 5-inch Peetz, and Allcock Aerialite (left to right).

difficult C. Chandler/Ballentine [Daily Double] Trophy in each year).

Another well-known guide was Ron Francis, former President of the Campbell River Guides Association. His prowess drew some famous clients, including John Wayne and Tommy Hunter. The Campbell River Museum houses a large collection of fishing tackle acquired from Ron. Its 1500 items amply illustrate the tackle used in the area. The Francis collection confirms that a great variety of reels were used locally. They include many Nottinghams and star-drag multipliers. The 5-inch Aerialite, which was manufactured by Allcock between 1930 and 1939, and again from 1949 to 1963, was clearly popular. One specimen (museum catalogue no. 988.26.25) bears the hand-written inscription "PR reel 23," indicating it once belonged with one of the boats at Painters Fishing Resort. The collection has a fine Canadian specimen, a robust 5-inch Bakelite reel with the auspicious name of Tyee (no. 988.26.24.); it was produced by Heard and Wilson Ltd. of Vancouver (Fig. 12.1).

The museum has two Peetz reels, a 6-inch (no. 988.26.22) and a 5-inch (no. 988.26.23), both of which were used by Ron Francis. The 5-inch shows some battle scars. Among numerous large fish taken on this reel, Ron recalled a 19-pound coho and a 31-pound tyee, both taken while bucktailing. His best tyee, the latter hangs in his tackle room. Ron added that he has caught much larger fish, but this one, taken on light tackle, put up the most memorable battle, taking angler and boat 4 miles north into Duncan Bay. At home, Ron has two more Peetz reels, still in use. For him, there is no reel to match the Peetz for reliability. The check on his reel is like a telephone to the world below: one click indicates weed on the line; two or three clicks speak of a suddenly frantic herring bait.

The town of Campbell River was also home to Roderick Haig-Brown. It provided the setting for many of his essays and arguments on conservation. The writings of Haig-Brown are among the most important in angling literature. They have done much to promote a conservation ethic among anglers, although it is probably fair to say that freshwater anglers have been more receptive to his message than their saltwater colleagues. But even before Haig-Brown settled in Campbell River and began to publish his books, a fishing ethic had begun to emerge among local anglers.

How and why the Tyee Club came into existence are well documented by Van Egan in *Tyee: the story of the Tyee Club of British Columbia* (essential reading for those interested in the club's history). In 1924, Messrs. Wiborn, Haigh, and Wolverton met in the Willows Hotel, Campbell River, to consider the future of the salmon and salmon fishing. Over the next few months, they and two others, John Asser and Walter Miller, drew up a code of conduct that in one stroke improved prospects for the salmon and the attractiveness of Campbell River for salmon fishing. They did this by restricting the type of tackle to be used, and the means by which the fish could be pursued and boated. A fish of 30 pounds or more meeting such restrictions made the angler eligible for membership in the Tyee Club of British Columbia. To put it simply, the Tyee Club made it more difficult to catch salmon. This helped the salmon. By increasing the challenge, the Club increased the prestige of success. This appealed to the angler.

In 1938, Ned and June Painter opened Painter's Lodge on a splendid site overlooking the mouth of the River. In the same year, the Tyee Club introduced a duplicate series of trophy buttons, awarded for fish caught under even more stringent rules of the Extra Light 3/6 Tackle Class (3/6 refers to the rod having a maximum length of 6 feet and weighing no more than 6 ounces, and a 6-thread line not exceeding 16-pound breaking strength). Initially, the Club discouraged inexperienced anglers from competing in the 3/6 Class by restricting entry to those who had earned the first three standard buttons, i.e. for 30-, 40-, and 50-pound fish; this restriction was eventually dropped. The 3/6 Class was discontinued in 1974, in an effort to simplify line weight regulations. The second largest fish ever taken under Club rules, a 70½-pound tyee, was caught by Ray Slocum in 1947 on 3/6 tackle.

The tyee challenge draws people from all over the world. Many are repeat contestants, bent on winning a coveted button. In the unpredictable waters off the river's mouth they discover the ultimate experience in saltwater salmon fishing. The simple yet stringent conditions they have accepted heighten the moment. The boat is quietly rowed in huddled company. The rod and line are light. An unbaited lure bears a single hook. Distractions are few: there are no downriggers, depth-sounders, or outboard motors. Concentration is paramount. The eye, hand, and mind must be tuned to the rod tip, ready for a telltale dip that heralds the

Fig. 12.2. The Tyee Club's Dr. Gavin Chisholm Trophy for best tyee caught on a single-action reel puts a 5-inch Peetz on a pedestal.

supreme reward.

Although the Tyee Club imposed limits on the length and power of rods and on the line used, the choice of reel was left open. Fixed-spool and star-drag multiplier reels were well developed when the Club was formed. But in retrospect, the omission of a reel restriction is somewhat surprising, given the advantages offered by a slipping clutch of the more complicated reels. It should be remembered, however, that a primary goal of the Club was to convert handliners to angling; the type of reel used was a minor consideration.

In 1968, Dr. Gavin Chisholm of Victoria gave the reel significance by awarding a trophy (Fig. 12.2) in his name for the largest tyee caught on a single-action reel. The trophy also imposed a reduced limit for line strength, but this was dropped in 1974 when the Club simplified tackle regulations.

The capture of a tyee was undeniably more challenging with a single-action reel. More important, its use further enhanced the fishing experience. Gavin Chisholm invited anglers to discover how simple tackle can increase the pleasure in trolling for salmon.

Peetz Manufacturing Ltd. received a fine endorsement from Gavin Chisholm, for his trophy consists of an elegantly mounted 5-inch reel made by the company. The largest fish to win the Trophy was a 62-pound tyee, taken by Tammy McKonkey of Campbell River in 1983. The trophy now residing at Painter's Lodge is not the original. The first one was lost on Christmas Eve, 1985, when fire completely destroyed the Lodge. The replacement reel bears Robertson screws in its handle-plates, a clear indication of more recent manufacture.

It may surprise some of today's tackle-conscious anglers that sophisticated and expensive tackle is not a prerequisite for catching big fish. Campbell River's most famous fish, Musgrave's 70-pound tyee, was caught over a century ago on a big Nottingham reel filled with linen line. No slipping clutches and gear clusters dulled the feel of that monster.

An enthusiast of fishing in the traditional manner, author Christopher Yates gives more food for thought in *Casting at the Sun,* published in 1986. He loves to fish with simple tackle. He demolished the myth of "high tech" tackle by landing a 51½-pound carp, Britain's biggest, on an ancient cane rod and an early Ambidex fixed-spool reel. But most of his fishing is done with old center-pins.

After the success of his book, Yates tried the medium of television. In the company of Bob James and wildlife photographer Hugh Miles, he produced an exquisite series of fishing films for the British Broadcasting Corporation under the title *A Passion for Angling*. The films conveyed the very essence of angling, with tongue-in-cheek banter among friends, a love affair with old tackle, and a reverence for fish and the waters they inhabit. The series touched a nerve in some angling circles, and the prices of old center-pins and cane rods quickly overtook modern wonders in bar-stock and graphite. Almost single-handedly, in the view of some, Yates has rekindled an appreciation for the finer points of angling, an appreciation that demands less from the fish and derives more from the self.

Yates has certainly helped to rekindle an interest in center-pins: the names of J.W. Young and Aerial have been resurrected with replicas of famous models of the past, and new reels bearing the names of Chris Yates and Bob James have appeared. A modern version of the Malloch Sidecaster is now offered as a refined center-pin that can be rotated through 90 degrees for casting. (Don't they remember that the Sidecaster twisted line at every cast?) This turn of events contrasts sharply with what has been happening on the West Coast. Peetz don't make replicas; they have just kept producing their Nottinghams through thick and thin, and there have been enough appreciative anglers to support them.

It is not my purpose here to advocate a return to the old style of angling, or to promote single-action reels over multipliers, or wire lines over downriggers for that matter. To each his own. But I am trying to illustrate that there are more dimensions to angling than bagging a limit of fish. The choice and use of tackle is one of them. Although it may kill more fish, modern sophisticated tackle does not necessarily add to the pleasures of fishing, and it may even detract from them.

I hesitated to discuss the issue in this book. I set out to chronicle a piece of angling history for the West Coast. But if the legend of the Peetz reel is to have a context, the salmon must survive. Our sport is utterly dependent on this creature. No angler with a conscience can duck the issue of the salmon's survival. Yet anglers are caught in hypocrisy. We expect others to make way for the salmon, by cleaning up forest practices, restricting mines, reducing energy needs, and so on. We argue on behalf of the salmon for clean waters, a lower commercial catch, and tighter surveillance on the high seas. Then we praise the salmon's fighting qualities. We fish to take our limit, and boast of our success. I am as guilty as the rest.

Joe Painter cured my hesitancy to explore the connection between tackle and conservation. The name Painter is synonymous with salmon fishing in Campbell River. Joe is one of the sons of Ned and June Painter, founders of the original Painter's Fishing Resort. Living at the mouth of the river most of his life, Joe has formed his own views on the future of the salmon.

I had gone to Joe for help on the connection between Campbell River and the Peetz reel. He agreed that it was a cosmopolitan mix of tackle that hung over the gunwales of his father's boats. Before and after the war, it was not unusual to see reels from Allcock, Hardy, Penn, Vom Hofe, and Peetz in a single morning. He showed me a battered Aerialite from the original Resort, this one inscribed with the number 36. But soon we fell into talk about the plight of the fish. He made point after point that reached to the very heart of the matter.

While rowing tyee, Joe Painter made some astute observations about his clients. "Simply put," he says, "people need to shine." Like hockey players and golfers, anglers are out to excel within the rules of the game. They want to return to the dock with an admirable fish. It does not have to be the best fish of the day, although that will add to the pleasure.

What the Tyee Club had done was to establish clear and stringent rules by which the fish should be caught. This did nothing to dissuade people from fishing the hard way. On the contrary, thousands of people have been enticed to Campbell River to try for salmon under the Club's standards. The King of Siam had to abide by the same rules as Joe's daughter Catherine. Van Egan tells us the King did not get his tyee during his visit in 1931. Some fifty-five years later Catherine took the Tyee Man, the ladies' Lillian J. Sparrow Trophy, and the Gavin Chisholm Trophy for 1986 with a single fish of 53 pounds.

Here, Joe made his next point. For people to accept the challenge of fishing by rules, there must be, in his words, "a level playing field." Every angler wants at least as good a chance as his or her fellow anglers.

Today the field is tilted in favor of the boat dressed in high technology. Trolling fresh bait from downriggers set at depths registering salmon on fish-finders, the high-power boat has an easy advantage over the rowboat. Joe remarked how a fishless but contented client suddenly can become disenchanted with the rower on seeing a large fish caught from a powerboat. Many clients come for fish, not fishing. Guides are inclined to provide their customers with what they want. It is good for business.

Joe pointed to the larger resorts, now offering powerboats far more numerous and effective than the dwindling rowboats. Many small operators add to the fleet, as do hundreds of local and visiting anglers. Pressure intensifies for fewer fish, and the possibility of a catastrophic collapse in the fishery looms larger. Meanwhile, resorts at Campbell River and elsewhere continue to promote fishing. They have to, with their millions, even tens of millions, of dollars invested in real estate and boats. They are vulnerable, but no more so than the salmon, on which they are so dependent.

In the interests of the salmon, the Tyee Club introduced a new button in 1983. The Catch-and-Release button is awarded for any chinook taken under Club rules and released. Joe has his doubts about releasing salmon. He is not persuaded by surveys that indicate a high rate of survival. For one thing, released salmon are tired, and highly vulnerable to seals. Joe is convinced that the only way to safeguard the salmon is to reduce the catch, not just the take. This does not apply solely to the commercial fishery. He maintains that, if we let it, the recreational fishery will take up whatever slack a reduced commercial fishery creates, at least in limited fisheries such as Campbell River. One concession Joe will agree to is the barbless hook. Any device that enables the angler to release the fish without delay is beneficial.

Mike Rippingale, guide and long-time friend of Joe, shares his concern, although he has his own philosophy when it comes to tackle. Acknowledging the threat of seals and other predators to tired fish, Mike argues for getting the fish in without delay. He questions the value the ultra-light tackle that prolong the fight unduly. "It's like shooting a moose with a .22," he says. While he prefers the single-action, he has seen too many guides exasperated by inexperienced clients with these reels in their hands. He advocates a return to star-drag multipliers under such circumstances. He speaks from experience. As Gavin Chisholm's guide and companion for many years, he recalled frustrating times, with big fish lost, as the good doctor struggled to master his beloved reel. Dr. Chisholm

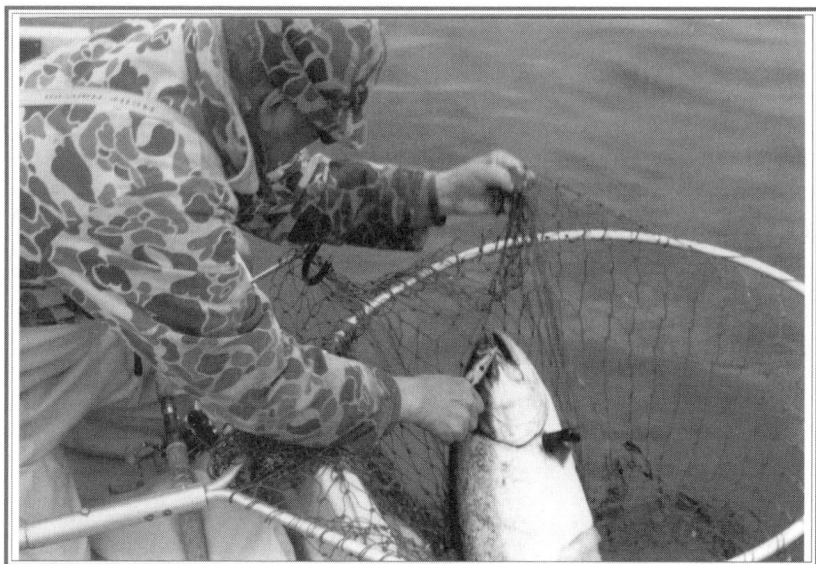

Fig. 12.3. A regular visitor to BC waters, Buck Nelson of Portland, OR uses barbless hooks for quick release of salmon.

The Campbell River Courier   Wed., Aug. 4, 1965

FIRST REGISTERED TYEE of the year is this 37 pounder caught by Dr. Gavin Chisholm of Victoria. A director of the Tyee Club of British Columbia, Dr. Chisholm took his tyee on 15 lb. test line from a rowed boat in the Tyee Pool guided by Mike Rippingale. Only salmon weighing over 30 pounds and caught according to the rigid rules of the famous Tyee Club are eligible for registration. The fish was weighed in at Painter's Lodge.

*Fig. 12.4. Dr. Gavin Chisholm with a hard-won tyee; reel is a Pflueger Sal-trout (*The Campbell River Courier, *August 3, 1965).*

would have controlled his tyee more easily with a Peetz reel than with the Pflueger Sal-trout he was using in 1965 (Fig. 12.4), for the Sal-trout had a totally caged drum, and hence lacked the all-important exposed rim through which pressure can be applied by hand.

Changes in attitude will not come about quickly. In the interim, we are obliged to promote the more tangible values of conserving our natural resources, but always at the risk of "selling out," of compromising the ultimate goal. We do not have to look far for measurable benefits. We have seen how the fortunes of the Peetz company have had to ride the crests and troughs of the West Coast fishery. The same is true for the twenty or so other Victoria companies, such as Scotty Plastics, Tomic Lures, and Radiant Lures, that manufacture fishing tackle. It is true for the hundreds of tackle shops, boat and marine suppliers, marinas, and fishing lodges that stretch from Sooke to Campbell River and beyond to the Charlottes. It all amounts to a lot of money and jobs. Whether the temporary closure in 1996 of chinook retention was necessary is debatable, but it revealed that an astonishing amount of wealth is dependent on this one species alone. Even though most lodges were able to survive the closure, it was costly for them.

We can express the value of recreation in terms of dollars spent and jobs created. But this does not give us a full evaluation. In the stress-ridden world of phones and faxes, bottom lines and deadlines, there is something to be said for fixing your senses on a gently nodding rod tip for a few hours. Left unattended, gray matter starts to sort the wheat from the chaff. It recreates order from chaos. It is hard to put a price on that.

Some argue that as the intelligent species we should rise above our primitive urges; we should not have to exploit other species for pleasure or profit. For me, the simplistic defense still holds: without the vested interest from anglers and hunters, the fish and wildlife of this planet would be in much worse condition than they are now.

Before leaving Campbell River I dropped in at Painter's Lodge. It was closed for the season but the winter staff kindly let me in to view trophies and photographs. There was an atmosphere about the place that had little to do with its plush decor. Perhaps it was the strong tide running outside in Discovery Passage. Painter's seems to be more a part of the water than it is of the land it sits on.

I was still looking for the Peetz connection. The Gavin Chisholm Trophy was hauled out of its cabinet for my camera. A 4-inch Peetz balanced a nice split-cane rod hanging over the doors of the upper gallery. The gallery was lined with framed photographs attesting to a glorious past. Among the more striking was a 1941 photograph of Mrs. T.B. Randall

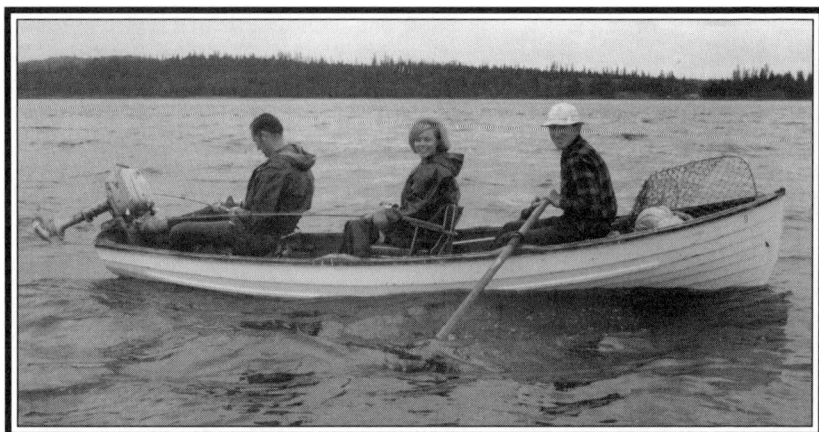

Fig. 12.4. Mike Rippingale rowing for a British Columbia promotional film in 1969.

with her record-breaking 66½-pound tyee (is the 6-inch Nottingham on her rod a Peetz?) Since 1941, Mrs. Randall's record has been officially beaten twice: first by Ray Slocum's 70½-pound fish taken in 1947, and then by a 71-pound fish caught by Walter Shutts in 1968.

Despite the decline in fishing at Campbell River, Painter's Lodge is guaranteed at least one sell-out event each year. It is the annual Women's Fishing Derby. You must book a year in advance to get in. Fish or no fish, the participants have the time of their lives. Many make reservations for the following year before they go home. They too have experienced the essence of fishing.

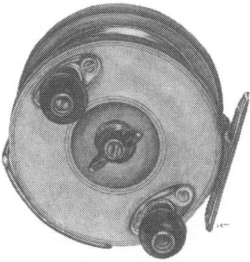

EPILOGUE

Seventy-three years have passed since Boris Peetz launched his Pacific reel. It was the start of an enterprise that would sustain two generations of his family for half a century. The second generation lives in busy and contented retirement in Victoria. Ola, Judy, Ivan, and Bud still love the water. Judy has built boats and sailed them. Ivan, as his father did, loves to tinker with machines, some of them quite substantial. Bud remains an active sailor.

Ola and Ivan each have family, five girls in all, and fourth and fifth generations are growing up. With five granddaughters now married, convention dictates that the name of Peetz is unlikely to be carried forward by the family. But as I look up from my keyboard I am quickly reminded that the name is alive and well. This book has been drafted under the watchful eye of a Peetz clock, presented to me by knowing colleagues on the occasion of my own retirement. This and other innovations, coupled with a steady demand for traditional reels, assures a place for the company for many years to come. And when the last wood reel is spun off the lathe, it will have several decades of life ahead.

When Boris and Edna came their separate ways to the West Coast, Victoria was still a pioneer town. Its streets bustled with miners and loggers. As they walked around the inner harbor they would have recognized the signs of a fine future. They built a new home, a family, and a business. They weathered the Great Depression. When they visited England after twenty years of struggling, the best was yet to come, for they were poised to create a legacy for the West Coast. Their company would be the most successful fishing tackle business in Canadian history.

The reel symbolizes the contribution made by the Peetz family. Anyone who uses a Peetz regularly will speak of it with a certain reverence. It may have been their first reel. Or it may have been passed on by a parent or grandparent. If so, it will have the marks of earlier encounters, of battles won and battles lost. Then there is its song. The sound of a reel is music to the angler's ear. Any reel sounds good as a big fish peels off

Fig. 13.1. Retrieved by divers after years on the ocean floor, these Peetz reels still turn, and their checks and drags still function.

Fig. 13.2. The ultimate test: almost consumed by a devastating boat fire, all moving parts of this Peetz still operate.

layer after layer of line. But the Peetz is built like a musical instrument; the rising crescendo of the check is amplified by the solid mahogany back-plate and resonates off the brass drum-plate. It is the sound of the reel I remember most about my first encounter with a chinook, over twenty years ago in Finlayson Arm.

Anglers appreciate fine, uncomplicated reels. Steve Raymond sums up the matter in *Steelhead Country* thus:

> *The best reels are works of art in cold metal, solid and strong, heavy and satisfying to the touch, with ever-sparkling polished brightwork. They are machines at rest, just waiting for a strong fish to start them running, and they have a look of action about them even when they are still.*

Boris Peetz would surely have agreed with these sentiments, but we cannot leave the last word with metal reels. Besides, Raymond was talking about fly reels.

For many anglers there is something else in the Peetz. Reflected in its mahogany drum, polished by a million turns against lead and planer, tide and fish, lies the glorious past of the West Coast. The reel has been an integral part of that past, a legend in its own time, as the saying goes. It has survived our adulation of the high priests of technology. Aside from the century-old Hardy Perfect, it is difficult to find a reel that has stood the test of time as well as the Peetz. Its course of evolution has been remarkably conservative. That is because a tough, uncomplicated design was found early in its history, and it suited the demanding conditions of West Coast trolling better than any other on the market. That advantage still holds. No other reel will take the abuse that the saltwater salmon angler can mete out. And if a Peetz reel does finally succumb, almost any damage can be repaired, although the factory has to draw the line occasionally (for examples, see Fig. 13.1 and 13.2).

The Peetz reel is an anachronism. Its classic form of mahogany and brass is of another age. To some it has no place among the paraphernalia of the modern salmon angler. But then even the modern angler is a bit of an anachronism. The Peetz extends across four generations. It is really something to be using your great-grandfather's reel.

The story of Boris Peetz extends across more than time. He was from another culture and another world. He was part of a great flood of humanity that ebbed and flowed across continents, pushed by poverty and desperation, drawn by hope and opportunity. He found a Canada bursting with exploration and enterprise, and he fitted it like a glove. He built fishing tackle that fitted the West Coast just as well. His initials, B.C., could not have been more appropriate.

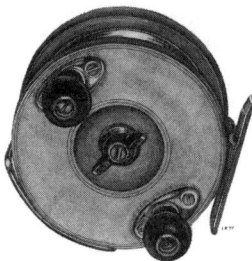

APPENDIX I

Maintenance and Renovation

With the right treatment, a Peetz reel will give its owner literally decades of use, and many thousands have done so. The nicest thing you can do for a saltwater reel is to rinse it in fresh water after each trip. All that is then required is an occasional cleaning and lubrication. Fly reels excluded, few get such luxurious treatment. Once a Peetz reel has been used it will show some corrosion.

How you set about refurbishing a reel depends on how it is to be used. Restoration of a Peetz for collection and display purposes can be daunting. It is probably no exaggeration to say that no other reel receives so much abuse. Once mounted on a rod and taken fishing, a Peetz may not see dry land again for many years. Continuous exposure to salt, prolonged cranking against heavy weights and large fish, and general neglect is tolerated by few reels. Yet this one can be virtually fused to the rod, its brass corroded to the point of disintegration, its lovely mahogany black with oil and dirt, and still catch fish! Boris Peetz expected no less of his reels, and he built them accordingly.

Some anglers send their reels back to the company every few seasons to have seriously worn or damaged parts replaced, an expedient not without merit. Nevertheless, the construction of a Peetz reel is simplicity itself. If corrosion has not been excessive, refurbishing is well within the capability of the average angler. Few tools are needed, and parts are easily obtained from the company, or even salvaged off irreparable reels.

Cleaning and lubrication

For basic maintenance, the reel can be dismantled with the aid of two or three screwdrivers. For older reels these will be for slotted screws only, and should be snug-fitting and hollow-ground if damage to the soft brass screws is to be avoided. Removal of handle-plates on newer reels requires the square-headed Robertson screwdriver; this causes some frustration outside Canada, where these handy screws are practically un-known. Phillips screws are used on current reels.

Begin with the lock screw on the spindle, noting that this has a conventional right-hand screw (clockwise to tighten), unlike most British Nottinghams, which use left-hand threads at this point. Spin off the wing nut, and remove the domed brass D-washer which slides along a flat at the end of the spindle. The underlying fiber washer may sit directly on the spindle sleeve of the drum, or it may be separated from it by a spring washer. As you draw off the drum, note whether washers are present underneath, and if so, carefully retain them. You are now in a position to decide whether to simply clean and lubricate the reel, or to proceed with some degree of renovation.

All exterior parts can be scrubbed with mild soap and water; an old toothbrush is ideal for this job. Inside, grease and oil should be washed away with kerosene or gasoline. Smear Vaseline or light grease over all interior brass, including the drum back-plate, the circular reinforcement of the back, and the check mechanism. Try to keep grease off the exposed wood. Oil the spindle, and reassemble if all components are in good condition. It may be desirable to add an extra spacing washer or two under the drum. The handles should not be oiled.

Renovation

Extending the fishing life of a reel may entail cleaning corroded brass and refinishing the wood. Reduce the drum to a workable level by removing the handles. Unless you have the skill and tools, do not attempt to remove the drum back-plate, for, in addition to the obvious set of five or more screws, it is held at the check gear by a flange of the spindle bush.

The brass back-plate is invariably corroded and may require extensive work with wet and dry emery cloth, followed by fine-grade (0000) steel wool. Do not begin with coarse abrasives or you will score the surface too deeply to be erased. Some discoloration will remain however carefully you work.

A similar approach can be taken with the wood surfaces of the drum, with wet and dry sand paper and steel wool. Alternatively, old varnish can be scraped away with a very sharp edge, such as a single-bladed razor; the resulting bare surface should be gently rubbed with fine steel wool. Take care not to erase the shallow concentric indentations on the drum. Domestic paint remover works well, but it may remove the original filler as well as varnish. When thoroughly dry, the wood should be given two coats of marine spar varnish. Allow the varnish to harden properly before the handles are replaced.

Renovation of the remaining parts of the reel presents rather more difficulty. The chief problem lies with the strap, which may be distorted as well as corroded. Many English Nottinghams that have been used for saltwater trolling suffered from heavy cranking under tension, which pulled the body of the reel back towards the rod butt, and bent the strap or foot in the process. The sturdier Peetz reels are less prone to such distortion, but reels will be found with a backwards lean. During the 1950s, the company acquired a "free-machining" brass,

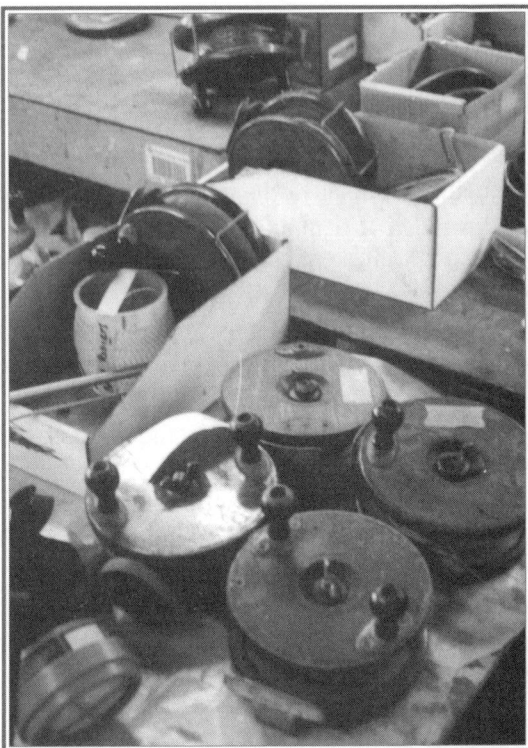

Fig. AI.2. A cluster of reels sent to the Peetz factory for servicing await their turn.

which was softer and easier to work, but resulted in bent straps.

Bill Hooson advises against correcting all but the most severe cases, as long as it does not interfere with normal operation of the reel. If correction is needed, it may entail removal of the strap, which is held by two or four brass machine screws. The exposed ends of these screws are usually burred; loosen nuts with care to avoid stripping threads. The offending bend in the strap must be straightened cold. If brass is reheated to redness it can be pushed back into shape with ease, but it will have lost its strength. It must be deformed cold in some way, such as rolling, if it is to regain its hardness. A better approach is to replace the strap completely.

Even if the strap is free of distortion, its removal will make cleaning and refinishing much easier. But given the ease with which screw heads and threads can be damaged, especially when corrosion has seized connections, it is often more prudent to work with the strap left in position. Cleaning of corroded metal and complete stripping of varnish will then become awkward, and the work will have to proceed more slowly. I have enjoyed some success with good quality rust remover for reducing surface corrosion, especially for oddly shaped surfaces, and for smaller items such as the check-plate that can be soaked separately. The brass reinforcement, inside the rim of the back-plate, can be removed, but the metal is thin and easily bent. It can be cleaned quite well when left in place. The line guard is easily removed, as long as the small screws are not burred. The check button will fall away when the inside mechanism is dismantled, exposing a bush set into the mahogany back-plate. It can be pushed out with the correct drift, but again, it is better left in place.

Some other metal components may need attention before being cleaned. Common problems include bent handle-plates, worn spindles, and broken line guards; sometimes these can be repaired rather than replaced. Some recent reels have had brass and wood components glued together; the laminated back-plate of the 1977 special 5¼-inch reel is a case in point. Such reels should not be soaked; if delamination does occur, the reel should be returned to the factory for repair.

Collection reels

Collectors of all kinds tend to be divided on the matter of cleaning and renovation. It would be hard to argue the merits of preserving untouched a badly corroded reel that has served a long and heavy sentence on an open boat in Sooke Harbor. The degree to which one should proceed with refurbishing such a reel, assuming that it has value to a collector, is debatable.

In theory, of course, the collector seeks the perfect specimen, free from serious blemishes, and therefore not in need of refurbishing. The theory works for freshwater reels, and if you have the money, an as-new hundred-year-old Hardy Perfect is yours for the asking. It doesn't work for Peetz reels, because they were built and bought as workhorses. In recent years, as wooden reels increasingly have become an anomaly, they have been used for trophies and presentations, suitably inscribed for recipients. But very few unused reels were put into collections, and that appears still to be the case. Consequently the collector is obliged to work with used reels and must confront the question of restoration.

Although I have placed some emphasis on the inevitability of corrosion, it is usually quite minor. Regrettably, in retrospect, I have passed up some rare early specimens on account of their corroded appearance. Brass is quickly tarnished by salt water, and almost inexorably verdigris begins to build. Once started it continues, even away from water, and should be stopped. A few hours of soaking in a 7 percent Calgon solution (a chelating agent) will help with removal of verdigris. Freshwater brushing and very light rubbing with the finest grade of steel wool available is effective; for stubborn patches, steel wool can be used in combination with good-quality rust remover. Look for 0000-grade steel wool for these jobs; the commonly available 000-grade is too coarse. Sometimes the cleaned metal will appear reddish in color, indicating a change in copper composition.

Bronze disease is an electrolytic process in which brass undergoes dezincification. Simply put, the zinc migrates out of the alloy, leaving porous copper behind. Whether bronze disease occurs in recent artifacts such as fishing reels is a moot point. Dealing with bronze disease and with corroding copper alloys in general is quite complicated. Some once-acceptable treatments are now known to involve carcinogenic chemicals. Sound advice usually can be obtained from the conservator of your local museum.

Whether to press on and completely restore the brasswork to brightness, with Brasso, for example, is a matter of choice that will depend on the extent of the corrosion, and on the importance you set by patina. There is a difference between corrosion caused by neglect and the patina brought about by slow oxidation. I was rather taken aback recently by a large case filled with fine old Nottinghams in an up-market shop in the English Cotswolds: every reel had been restored, with its walnut and brasswork gleaming. They formed an impressive, not to mention expensive, display but I could not help wondering whether value had been subtracted rather than added by the hard work. Many manufacturers blued the brasswork on their reels, and the extent of original bluing can be an important measure of a reel's condition. It is perhaps fortunate that the original brasswork of Peetz reels was left bright (except on the all-metal "2000" model).

The wooden components of Peetz reels were finished with several coats of marine varnish. Although very resilient, the varnish deteriorates over time and should be replaced. Fine-grade steel wool will remove flaking varnish, and if used with persistence will strip all the varnish, leaving a smooth surface that can be refinished. Varnish should be used in very thin coats. Thick coats will leave the reel with an all-too-evident refinished appearance which may be acceptable for outdoor use, but would certainly mar the appearance of a collection reel.

Wood needs careful handling in collection reels. Occasionally I have completely stripped worn walnut Nottinghams, and refinished them with French polish; it is a rather time-consuming procedure but the resulting depth of color imparted to the wood grain can restore an apparently hopeless case to a thing of beauty, albeit departing somewhat from the original finish. Where the reel is only lightly marked, an attractive matte finish can be achieved by gently scoring the varnish and any exposed wood with the finest steel wool, and finishing with well-rubbed French polish.

Appendix II

Collector's Guide

Over the past few years I have scoured Vancouver Island auction halls, antique malls, and flea markets for particular specimens of the Peetz reel series, with only moderate success. In doing so I have noticed that those I pass up are usually gone by my next visit. Some may be destined for more active service, but I suspect that most are going into collections. I also suspect that some buyers, especially visitors from more distant parts, see in them a bargain, for other wood reels are fetching high prices these days. As authors Harold Jellison and Dan Homel wrote in their recent book on antique reels, "Peetz reels are often mistaken for older British antiques (such as the 19th century Nottingham wood reel), so be careful—these neat looking high quality Peetz reels are still being produced and many are not very old." *Caveat emptor* indeed! Their illustrated guide is the first I have seen to feature a Peetz reel, a further sign that collectors are on the move.

The vast majority of second-hand reels have been used on salt water, and show the signs. It is axiomatic for the collector to look for the least corroded specimens, and by and large, the condition is readily apparent. But there are a number of less obvious pitfalls to bear in mind.

Most reels come packed with line, and this may hide problems underneath, such as a damaged or distorted drum back-plate. Corrosion is usually at its worst under old line. Occasionally the mahogany back-plate may be split, yet the defect may remain almost invisible because the strap continues to hold the two pieces tightly together. The problem is more prevalent among reels that have been stored in drier climates, especially east of the Rockies.

Many reels have been repaired at some time or other, and contain factory but not original components. The most common replacements are handles: occasionally they differ in size from the original, and recent

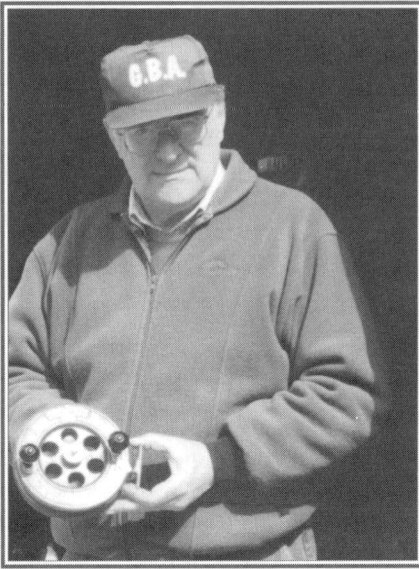

Fig. AII.1. Barry Degg of G.B. Angling, Scarborough, England holds one of the only mahogany Scarboroughs made by Seareels. At this time the Peetz remain the last known Nottinghams in production world wide.

replacements have plastic knobs. Most extendible arms were retrofitted, leaving exposed screw holes from the original handle-plate. The screws themselves are useful guides, not only to the age of reels, but also as indicators of replacement parts, for Robertson screws are now used in most applications.

The label, if present, is a useful but not wholly reliable guide to age. It was common for the factory to use up old labels after a change in ownership or address. Old labels have even been acquired from the factory in the past, and stuck onto reels during refinishing. But for the most part the label, or even a fragment of it, provides a valuable quick indication of age.

Although Boris Peetz may have built his first reel as early as 1924, examples of the initial period of evolution, say the first ten years, are extremely hard to find. Even the full-fledged Pacific Recorder that was making waves up and down Saanich Inlet in the 1930s is elusive. Most of the time the collector will have to be content with examples from the postwar era, and rejoice should any earlier material fall his or her way.

A basic collection would include examples of the three common sizes, 4, 5, and 6 inches, noting that these are nominal sizes only, and vary according to date. More effort will be needed to find specimens with the riveted and soldered foot, common to all reels built before the big press began stamping out the strap and foot in one piece in 1960. The 6-inch could be represented by both a standard and a Recorder model. As noted earlier, 5-inch Recorders are very hard to find. Beyond that, the 6¾-inch

Fig. AII.2. The ultimate find for a collector, this Scarborough-style Pacific is the earliest known Peetz reel. This Pacific Reel surfaced in a Victoria garage sale just before this book went to press.

Y-strap Recorder is a choice piece, as is the later 6¾-inch straight-strap Recorder, both featuring aluminum indicator discs.

Among more recent models, the 5¼-inch Recorder made in 1977 is a nice addition, if you can find one, and the two early metal reels provide interesting forerunners of the "2000". The 65th Anniversary edition is still fairly plentiful, having been built in a run of about 7000; I have yet to see (or smell) the reputed camphor wood model. For those with a botanical or forestry bent, a collection of reels featuring the different woods used can make an interesting series in its own right, but you will need to hone your skills of identification, for at times Boris used whatever timber could be found. A word of warning: Peetz reels are big reels, and they take up much more space than fly reels. You quickly run out of mantel shelf. But my wife prefers to have the Peetz collection over all others for display in the public areas of our house.

Of course, every collector has special places to search for elusive specimens. Vancouver Island is still a "happy hunting ground" for tackle collectors, but it takes hard work and persistence to find what you are looking for. Fellow collectors surprise me with what they turn up at garage sales and flea markets, but frankly I prefer to spend such time as that takes in other pursuits, such as fishing. Vancouver Island has many antique shops and malls, regular flea markets and auction houses, and they are all potential sources. The mainland of British Columbia, too, has similar places to visit, but, as on the Island, there are vigilant collectors everywhere.

Canadians are viewed by their neighbors to the south as "closet collectors," and the label fits. American collectors are much more visible, with exhibitions and "swap and shops" geared to the tackle collector. There seem to be many more dealers specializing in old fishing tackle in Washington and Oregon antique malls than we have in Canada. There is also more going on by mail order and, lately, by Internet. Interestingly, Peetz reels appear to be more highly valued in the United States than in Canada, but maybe that is just part of the Canadian condition. As collectibles, Peetz reels, and other items of tackle under this label, are still in their infancy, but a mounting interest in the history and artifacts of angling in the Pacific Northwest will almost certainly change this. In the meantime, there is an opportunity to build a representative collection of these classics at a reasonable price.

At the end of this section I have tabulated the main events in the development of the Peetz company and its reels. Because they were handmade, and the maker had some discretion in final finish and even choice of components, no two reels are identical. Likewise, no two pieces of wood are identical, adding to the immense variety to be encountered. But beyond essentially cosmetic diversity there are definite stages in evolution to be discerned, along with some uncommon forms, and acquiring examples of these to create a representative collection provides an interesting and fulfilling pursuit for those days when the wind is too strong or the river too high for fishing.

If I have one concern about this book it is that I may have missed some important stages in the evolution of the reel. To my knowledge no comprehensive collection exists, but I shall be happy to be corrected on that. A museum display recognizing the importance of sport fishing in British Columbia is long overdue. At the time of writing, a museum of fly fishing is being developed in Kamloops, but the need to cover other elements of the sport, especially West Coast salmon fishing, remains. When it comes, I have no doubt that the contribution made by the Peetz company will be more widely appreciated. In the meantime, I hope this book provides a reasonably reliable starting point for the collector and piques the interest of enthusiasts of the history of salmon fishing in British Columbia.

Summary of the Development of Peetz Reels

Year(s)	Event and Indicator
1924	Probable first year reels were sold Scarborough style; wood drum mounted on brass bracket Some brackets stamped with "The Pacific Reel"
1925–c1930	Nottingham style adopted All-wood drum, mounted on wood back-plate Followed by introduction of brass rear drum-plate
c1933–48	6¾-inch Pacific Recorder Y-strap on back-plate Single thick aluminum indicator disc Crown-shaped check spring Handle-plate flat
c1935	B.C. Peetz Manufacturing Company moved into rental premises at 572 Johnson Street
c1938	Company relocated to 574 Johnson Street
1939–45	World War II Uncertain production Woods other than mahogany may be evident
1947	Company expanded into a family business Diamond-shaped labels read "Peetz and Son" Handle-plate raised to accommodate retaining nut
c1949	Y-strap replaced by straight strap Aluminum indicator disc in two pieces Butterfly check spring introduced Recorder reels available in 5-(rare), 5¾-, and 6¾-inch diameters Standard reels available in nominal 4-, 5-, 6-, and 6¾-inch diameters
c1953	Plastic indicator disc introduced 6¾-inch reels discontinued Reel sizes reduced to 3¾, 4¾, and 5¾ inches
1954	Boris Peetz died 12 January 1954, age 70
1958	Check button no longer perforated by screw
1959	Acquisition of punch press
1960	Strap and foot formed in single pressing

1967	Company changes its title from Peetz and Son to Peetz Tackle Ltd.
1973	Company split retailing business from manufacturing Factory moved to Rock Bay Avenue Diamond-shaped label reads "Peetz Manufacturing Ltd.," but Company is listed in 1973 only as Peetz Tackle Manufacturing Ltd.
1976	Narrow-drum 5¼-inch Recorder produced in small numbers
1977	Company sold to Bill Hooson and renamed Peetz Manufacturing (1977) Company Diamond-shaped label replaced with "Peetz" insignia burnt into wood Slot-head screws replaced by Robertson screws Reel models numbered: 4-inch: 1400; 5-inch: 1500; 6-inch: 1600; 6-inch Recorder: 2500
1979	Plastic handles phased in
1980	First metal reel (5-inch) introduced, with coated brass finish Metal reels discontinued after failure of finish to resist corrosion
1982	Metal reel reintroduced with nickel plating finish Production stopped after failure of plating
1990	4-, 5-, and 6-inch reels produced in 65th Anniversary editions
1995	Metal "2000" reel (5-inch) introduced
1996	Reel clocks (5-inch) introduced
1997	Fly-reel clocks (3½-inch) introduced

BIBLIOGRAPHY

Anon. 1932. "Brentwood's great fighting salmon lure fishermen from afar; chinook buttons for big ones now the rage in sports honours." *Victoria Daily Times*, August 6, 1932: p. 5

Anon. 1954. "Fish lure inventor Boris Peetz passes." *Victoria Daily Times*, January 13, 1954: p. 2.

Bingham, D. 1997. "Property watch." *Trout and Salmon*. May 1997: p. 32.

Crankshaw, E. 1976. *The shadow of the Winter Palace: the drift to revolution 1825-1917*. Macmillan London Limited, London. 429 pp.

Egan, V.G. 1988. *Tyee: the story of the Tyee Club of British Columbia*. Ptarmigan Press, Campbell River, British Columbia. 208 pp.

Evans, H. 1979. "Day of the hand troller." *Pioneer days in British Columbia*. Heritage House. 4: 58-63.

Falkus, H., and F. Buller. 1994. *Falkus and Buller's Freshwater Fishing*. Grange Books, London. 525 pp.

Fedoruk, E. 1985. "Peetz reels are Canadian classics." Victoria *Times Colonist*, June 21: p. B3.

Gregson, H. 1970. *A history of Victoria 1842-1970*. J.J.Douglas Ltd., Vancouver, B.C. 246 pp.

Jellison, H., and D.B. Homel. 1996. *Antique and collectible fishing reels: identification, evolution and maintenance*. Forest Park Publishers, Bellingham, Wa. 192 pp.

Lee, Philip, 1996. *Home pool: the fight to save the Atlantic Salmon*. Goose Lane Editions, Fredericton, NB. 279 pp.

Musgrave, R.J. 1896. "A seventy pound salmon with rod and line." *The Field*. Harmsworth Press, London. Vol. 88, October 24, 1896.

Obee, B. 1995. "Saanich Inlet." *Beautiful British Columbia*. 37: 6-17.

Orrelle, J. 1987. *Fly reels of the past*. Frank Amato, Portland, Ore. 155 pp.

Raymond, S. 1991. *Steelhead country*. Lyons and Burford, New York. 200 pp.

Stephenson, J. 1994. *Rosewood to revolution: the development of the centrepin fishing reel*. John Stephenson, Stoke-on-Trent, England. 287 pp.

Temple, L. G. 1951. "Fun in the reel business." Vancouver *Sun* (Magazine), July 14, 1951: p. 14

Turner, G. 1989. *Fishing tackle: a collector's guide*. Ward Lock Ltd., London. 384 pp.

Wilson, C. 1997. "Peetz reels in alarming sales." Victoria *Times Colonist*, March 1, 1997: p. E1.

Wormald, R. 1952. "Harbour lights." *Daily Colonist* (Magazine), Victoria, B.C. October 22, 1952: p. 3.

Wormald, R. 1953 "Harbour lights; Peetz and Son." *Daily Colonist*, (Magazine), Victoria, B.C. March 1, 1953: p. 8.

Yates, C. 1986. *Casting at the sun: the reflections of a carp fisher*. Pelham Books, London. 232 pp.

INDEX

Douglas F.W. Pollard

At the age of 12 Doug Pollard cast a line into the River Mole and never looked back. A few years later he was lured by the fishing prospects offered by the University of Wales, Aberystwyth, and collected a Ph.D. in botany. After two years working as a wildlife biologist at the Wildfowl Trust in Slimbridge ("actually being paid to be on the water"), he emigrated to Canada to develop a career in forest research ("and to do a bit more fishing").

Initially specializing in the physiology of tree growth, he pressed his concerns over conservation and deteriorating environments. For several years he was Senior Policy Advisor, Environment, for Forestry Canada, and represented forestry on the Canadian Council on Ecological Areas. He established himself as a leading authority on the implications of climate change, and in 1987 delivered the E.B. Eddy Distinguished Lecture, Forestry and Climate Change: Facing Uncertainty. He has published over 75 papers in scientific and professional journals. He celebrated his retirement in 1996 by catching a 262 lb. halibut off Langara Island.

Forty-five years of fishing have taken the author to many exotic destinations, but he still prefers to fish his local waters, wherever they may be. Thirty years in Canada have increased his appreciation of and concern for wild fish stocks, in both fresh- and saltwater. Doug is a member and Past-President of the Haig-Brown Fly Fishing Association in Victoria, where he lives with his wife Penny. Fishing remains paramount, but he continues to write, mostly about fish and fishing. There is a modest collection of antique tackle that he wishes he had started earlier, or never started at all.

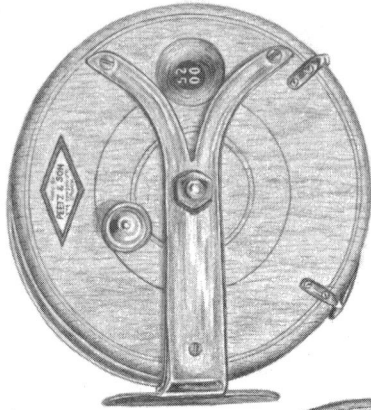

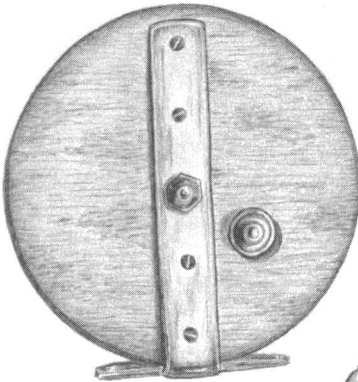

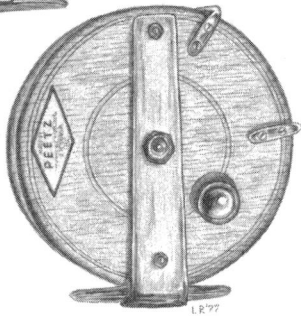

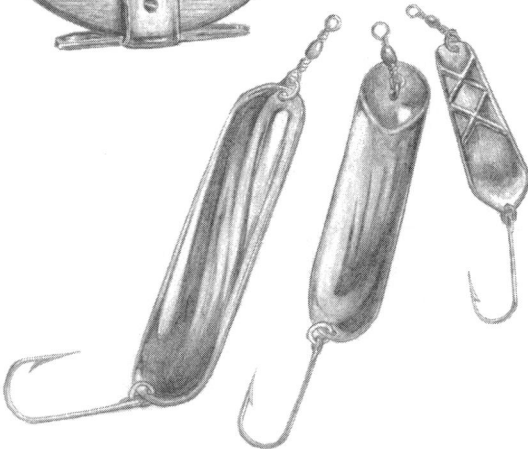